ENDORSEMENTS

Rarely in life do we see apostles up close and personal. Though he would probably deny it, PG Vargis is an apostle in every sense of that biblical term. Here is his story. Enjoy!

—Dr. Paul Leming
Founding Pastor, St. James United Methodist Church
Founder, Barnabas Project, Tulsa, Oklahoma

PG Vargis is a great man of God who has done a tremendous job of reaching not only his own people in India, but many in other nations as well. John loved him like a son, and our family salutes him. This book will bless multitudes.

—Dodie Osteen
Co-Founder, Lakewood Church, Houston, Texas

First-century apostolic Christianity is alive and well in the twenty-first century! The story of Dr. PG Vargis reads like something from the book of Acts. I don't know anyone who is doing more to advance the kingdom of Christ than my dear friend, Dr. Vargis.

—Brian Zahnd
Pastor, Word of Life Church, St. Joseph, Missouri

I have known PG Vargis for many years. His story and testimony have been a great inspiration and encouragement to me.

—Charles M. Duke, Jr.
Apollo 16 Lunar Module Pilot

I met PG Vargis over twenty-five years ago on my second trip to India. I have since visited his home and work many times, and he has ministered in our church in Japan. He is a dear friend and one of the hardest-working and most trustworthy men I have ever met. His story is an inspiration and encouragement to all who are willing to risk it all for the sake of the kingdom.

—Ricky Gordon
Missionary-Pastor, Living Way Church
Shizuoka-shi, Japan

From a soldier in the Indian Army to a veritable general among missionaries working in the most distant parts of India, PG Vargis has been an inspiration to an entire generation of Indian Christians. His testimony and that of his wife, Lilly, have given strength and hope to members of a persecuted church. This couple's success is a tangible sign of God's design for India.

—Dr. John Dayal
Member, National Integration Council,
Government of India; National President (2004–08),
All India Catholic Union, representing 16 million
Catholics in India's 155 dioceses

As supplier of the large quantities of scriptures ordered by Dr. PG Vargis for use in the ministry of IET, I can surely say that he is an esteemed partner in helping distribute the Word of God throughout India. Dr. Vargis, founder and chief mentor of IET, is, by example, worthy of the honor that is being bestowed on him through the writing of this book about his life and ministry and the ensuing ministry of Indian Evangelical Team.

—Richard G. Khan
Auxiliary Secretary, Bible Society of India
New Delhi, India

PG Vargis is a pioneer Indian missionary who can rightly be called a modern apostle. The story of his life, an adventure in faith, will inform and inspire many. I highly recommend this compelling story of faith, hope, and compassionate love—the story of an obedient life in unselfish service to the kingdom of God.

—Dr. Thomson K. Matthew
Dean, School of Theology and Missions,
Oral Roberts University, Tulsa, Oklahoma

A unique and respected leader among leaders, PG Vargis is a visionary and pioneer—a man of conviction and commitment to the call of God to reach the lost in India. I have been privileged to know him for more than thirty-two years, and I've witnessed the great impact his ministry has made for Christ in India. I am sure you will enjoy this book about the life and ministry of PG Vargis and his family.

—Thomas Samuel
Founder-President, Quiet Corner India
Former Coordinator of Operation Mobilisation

Over the years, I have admired the grace of God evidenced in the apostolic ministry of PG Vargis. Truly he is one of the pioneers in the astonishing harvest into the kingdom of God, which we are seeing at this present time.

—Patrick Johnstone
WEC International, Wisbech, England

PG Vargis is truly a man of faith who heard the call of God and set out like Abraham. Through PG's vision and leadership, hundreds of churches have been planted in some of the most difficult areas of North India, and thousands have come to a saving knowledge of our Lord Jesus Christ. May the Lord make this book a blessing for many, just as He has made this faithful servant a blessing to thousands!

—George Chavanikamannil
President and Founder: Good News for India,
La Verne, California; New Theological College &
Christian Evangelistic Assemblies, Dehra Dun, India

...TO SHARE HIS LOVE

...TO SHARE HIS LOVE

How the Love of God Touched One Man —and Changed a Nation

DR. PG VARGIS

Published by HonorNet
P.O. Box 910
Sapulpa, OK 74067
Web site: honornet.net

Author Contact Information:

US Postal: GET
             P.O. Box 702411
             Tulsa, OK 74170

Website: www.getmissions.org
             www.pgv.com

Email: pgvargis@pgv.com

DEDICATION

This book is dedicated to the Master, who called me out
of the Indian Army and made me what I am today—
His committed servant. To Him be the glory!

IN MEMORY OF

This book is released in memory of my good friend Jim Kerby.
Jim was a true friend and brother who loved the nation of India as if it
were his own country. His deep regard and love for the Indian people and
his belief in the work of IET served as a catalyst in getting the message,
passion, and story on these pages. Even in Jim's final days before going
to be with the Lord, he was concerned with making sure that his sister,
Norma Collins, would continue this work until it was complete.
Thanks, Jim, for believing in us and for allowing God to compel
you to love us, your brothers and sisters in India. Many seats
at the banquet table are reserved because of your love.

Your brother and friend,
PG

From the Publisher

WE MEET HUNDREDS OF PEOPLE DURING OUR LIFETIME. MANY are mere acquaintances who pass by with little more than a mannerly salutation. A few we remember, and others we barely notice. Some are in our lives for a short season, others for a lifetime. Then there are those rare occasions when God brings into our lives a divine appointment. We meet someone He purposefully guides across our path, if only for a moment, to bring clarity, direction, and impact that marks our lives forever. My first and only personal contact to date with PG Vargis was such an encounter.

PG was in my town and on his way to the airport to return to India, when a last-minute meeting was arranged for us in a mutual friend's home. Though I don't remember his exact words, PG asked what led or qualified me to be in publishing. My answer surprised even me. I blurted out, "Nothing. I'm not qualified. I can only believe that for some reason God trusts me." With tears in his eyes, PG looked at me and whispered, "I'm not qualified either."

I knew very little of PG before that twenty-minute conversation, but our short encounter was a divine appointment that marked me. God affirmed that He is more interested in our passion and availability than in our qualifications and intentions. I was driven not to be the publisher, but to be close to something that was near to the heart of God.

While I was working on the manuscript, God woke me one morning and seared into my spirit two things. The first was that the title of this book, *Compelled*, is actually a message for all of us. We have added to and done so much in the name of Christ that we have lost sight of the single, most important power behind Christianity—His love. Christ's love is the most powerful force in the universe. His love should be our sole motivation as we are Christ's hands extended to the world.

The second thing was concerning India herself. India is physically located on the frontlines of the world's economic, political, and cultural battlefields. For thousands of years, her soil has been stained with the blood of those who have fought for her land and sought her natural resources. Centuries before the birth of Christ, Alexander the Great counted the region of Punjab one of his greatest conquests. Now, two thousand years after Christ's birth, the fiercest battle in the history of India is being waged. It is the battle for India's greatest treasure—the heart and soul of her people.

God is the author of time and knew this battle would be raging in the present hour. Over thirty years ago, He planted a seed in a man's heart to share the love of Christ with his fellow countrymen. Today that seed has grown and matured, with other planted seeds, as is evidenced in the lives of the thousands of men, women, and children who have been reconciled to their Creator. Countless others still wait to feel His love.

As this battle rages, our Indian brothers and sisters have come under severe persecution for their faith. The burning of their homes and churches has left thousands homeless and living in the forests simply because they have given their hearts to Christ.

Just as India plays a pivotal role in the physical world, it holds a significant position in the spiritual realm. We must allow the love of Christ to compel us to join our faith, prayers, and means to India. Her very soul lies in the balance.

Jake Jones
Publisher, HonorNet

ACKNOWLEDGMENT

GRATEFUL THANKS TO THE HUNDREDS OF PASTORS AND WORKERS who daily put their lives on the line by sharing the gospel in India.

CONTENTS

PREFACE

In 1972, God called my wife, Lilly, and me to serve as pioneer missionaries in Katra, then a totally unreached, hostile Hindu pilgrimage town, located in the lower Himalayan Mountains. Having been disinherited by our families for obeying God's call on our lives, we had no regular source of income and often went hungry. But believing that everyone has a right to hear the gospel at least once, we dedicated our lives to taking that message to the lost souls of India.

That was the beginning of our mission, and in those early years, God brought others who shared our vision of reaching the unreached with God's love. By 1977, we had been blessed with enough workers to form a team, which we called Indian Evangelical Team, or IET. As their leader, I was grateful to work alongside these passionate and dedicated believers who, like Lilly and I, had surrendered their lives to the call of God to minister in India.

The team grew rapidly during the next few decades, and I trained many leaders not only to minister but also to oversee the planting of hundreds of churches across India. As we moved to obey God's call, we saw large numbers of lost souls respond to the gospel. The results were truly amazing.

In May 2004, as a memorial to the next generation, I took IET leaders back to Katra, where the long journey had started, and told them the tales of our humble beginnings. I reiterated IET's foundational values and God-given mission by recounting my personal testimony, as well as some of the other stories that I now share with you in this book.

I pray that as you read these accounts, you will rejoice with us at the great things the Lord has done . . . and share our heartbreak and distress over those who are still lost and dying without the hope of the gospel message. In addition, I pray that you will be touched by God's yearning for South Asia and that you will join us through prayer and support in reaching the unreached with His love.

ONE IN A BILLION

"Whoever receives one such child in My name receives Me."
Matthew 18:5

T HERE WAS SHOPPING TO DO, AND MY WIFE, LILLY, AND I HAD heard about a weekly market in a nearby village where people from the smaller surrounding villages converged to buy their goods. Eager to share the gospel message whenever and wherever we could, we decided to go there and preach, and then buy some vegetables for the week. So we gathered our children and walked to the market.

The first thing that strikes most visitors to India is its burgeoning population and the accompanying noise that is generated by vast numbers of people. Jillions of bicycles and motorcycles, each with three and four people hanging on precariously, weave in and out of traffic. Horns blare and cars pass other vehicles with reckless abandon as they swerve along decaying roads.

Our experience that day was quite similar. There in the village, teeming masses of people jostled us from every side. Unfamiliar sights, sounds, and smells assaulted our senses. Sheep, goats, and cattle wandered about aimlessly, their bleating cries and mournful lows merely adding to the overall cacophony.

Clambering onto a large rock, I looked around to gain my bearings. As I gazed out over the throng, compassion gripped my heart. I called to my wife and pulled her up beside me.

"Lilly, how many people do you see?" I asked.

"Who could count them all?" she responded, staring in dismay at the myriad of faces.

I pressed further. "Lilly, how many people are wearing anything on top?"

After several moments of careful searching, she answered, "I see only three."

All at once, the magnitude of poverty overwhelmed me, and I found I could no longer contain my emotions. I wept. To think that the majority of those who were scurrying about below me conducted all of their social and business activities in nothing more than a loincloth!

As I continued to survey the river of people before me, I spotted a young woman—a tribal, maybe twenty years old—sitting with a basket between her legs so that no one could snatch it. Her eyes were glazed over as if she were looking but not seeing.

I pointed out the girl to Lilly. Then I slid from the rock and turned to help Lilly down, explaining, "I want to take a picture of her for the newsletter."

The closer I drew to the spot where the poor girl was sitting, the clearer her situation became. There was no life in her eyes, just a dull, vacant stare. I could tell she was not married because she didn't wear a nose ring, the sign of a married woman. But it was her demeanor that told the real story and portrayed the obvious—she had been abused by many men.

I am Indian, so I understand the culture well. I knew this young woman had not given her body to men for pleasure. She had done it for the money. Not for herself, but for a younger brother or sister, or perhaps for a sick mother.

Deeply touched by the girl's haunting stare, I thought, *How many more are out there just like her? How many millions are dying without hope, without help, without salvation?*

As I turned to walk away, I was consumed with a deep burden and a keen awareness of the urgent need for the gospel to be preached across the vast, diverse land of my birth. How many others who had experienced a similar tragedy were just existing day to day, with no hope for a better tomorrow?

"Did you get a picture?" Lilly asked when I returned to her side.

I choked back my tears. "Yes, I got the picture," I said. "But not with the camera. Her picture is in my heart."

Chapter 1

GOD'S CALL TO THE MOUNTAINS

"Everyone therefore who shall confess Me before men, I will
also confess him before My Father who is in heaven."
Matthew 10:32

I T WAS CHRISTMAS WEEK 1971. LILLY AND I WERE SITTING ON A ROCK after our usual evening walk through the barren hills outside the army camp in Kashmir, where I was stationed as a soldier in the army. As we sat in the silence of the majestic, snow-capped Himalayan Mountains, we experienced an overwhelming sense of God's presence and began to worship Him. Then, as our worship subsided, a spontaneous prayer fell from Lilly's lips, a familiar and continual experience for her. Because I was a brand-new Christian, I was not yet as adept at expressing myself in prayer as Lilly was. Though my prayers were quite acceptable to the Lord, they consisted of short, halting words. I marveled at Lilly's beautiful and eloquent prayers that flowed from her heart.

As twilight fell, I watched the flickering light of first one small fire and then several others. Then twenty, forty, sixty, seventy-five—the fires stood like match flames all along the far-reaching mountainside. As far as the eye could see, the hills were inhabited by mountain people who lived in the basins. During the monsoon season, water flowed down the hills and made the valleys suitable for cultivation. The people who inhabited these regions were farmers, illiterate and uneducated. They lived in mud houses and subsisted on the crops they raised in the fertile valleys. In the daytime these people were virtually invisible, but in the evenings their presence was silently announced by the fires they lit in their courtyards as they cooked their evening meals.

That evening, while watching hundreds of these dinner fires spark to life across the face of the mountain, I interrupted my wife's prayer. "Lilly, do you see the flames of the cooking fires on those faraway mountains?"

"Yes, of course," she answered, "we see them every night."

Suddenly struck by a sobering sense of injustice, I said, "Do you realize that behind every fire, there's a family of five or ten who have never heard about Christmas?" My voice trembled with emotion. "Don't you think they should hear the story of Christmas at least once?"

Thinking of the perilous nature of traversing the Himalayan Mountains, Lilly responded, "But who will go? The mountains are hard to navigate, and they're filled with all kinds of danger. It would take a lifetime to climb so many hills! Who could withstand such an ordeal?"

"Lilly, we can!" I persisted. "We can be missionaries to these mountain people."

"It's just not possible," she protested. "They speak different languages and have customs we know nothing about. Even if we were able to reach them, we wouldn't be able to communicate with them. Their hearts would be hard—and besides, there's no financial security in missionary work."

"Maybe we could give them a book," I ventured, searching for a solution.

"But they can't read!" she countered.

"Maybe I could act out the message. Surely we could do *something*," I said. Desperate to make her understand what I was feeling in my heart, I grasped her by the shoulders and continued. "We could go into one village and share the gospel, and when somebody there becomes a Christian, we could go on to the next village and help someone there become a Christian. Then those converts could take the message to the surrounding villages. Why, in a few years, we could take all of India for Christ!" The very thought of it thrilled my heart.

With shocked emotions bordering on anger, Lilly threw my arms from her shoulders. "No!" she exclaimed. "We would be forced to live in poverty, and we would be persecuted and shunned. Besides, we are from South India. We could never withstand the brutal cold of the winters in the north. I have trained to be a teacher, not a missionary."

As a new Christian, my heart was burning with red-hot zeal to share the story of Jesus with those who had never heard it. So I implored, "But think what it would mean to the people. I heard the gospel once, and it changed my life!"

Driven by an unrelenting passion to share the good news of Christ with the mountain villagers, I squeezed her hands and kept pleading with her. "Lilly, the world has been celebrating Christmas for nearly two thousand years. In a few days, you and I will again be celebrating the birth of our Lord Jesus. Shouldn't those families hear at least once about the Savior who was born on Christmas Day? At least once, Lilly!" I cried. The insistence in my voice surprised even me.

Finally my words pierced her heart, and she began to cry. "Yes, of course they have the right to hear at least once about Christmas. If you go, I will go with you. But it will be difficult and dangerous. You know as well as I do that the mountains are rugged and treacherous. Our feet will bleed, and we'll have nothing to protect us from the bitter cold."

"God will be with us," I assured her.

We clasped our hands together and prayed as we looked toward the cooking fires in the distant, far-flung villages of the Himalayan Mountains. At that moment, we surrendered to the mighty call of God and committed our lives to missionary service. Willing to do whatever was necessary no matter the cost, we were indeed *compelled* to take the gospel to the unreached people of North India.

Do You See What God Sees?

How do you view the people you come in contact with each day? Do you make it a point to see past their outward appearance and to notice how they're really doing?

Jesus always took the time to look beyond the external, to see individuals as His heavenly Father saw them—through eyes of compassion. Matthew 9:36 tells us that Jesus was actually *moved with compassion*, for the people were *weary and scattered, like sheep having no shepherd* (NKJV). So even when viewing the multitudes, Jesus saw straight to the heart of the need. He understood that only through His death and resurrection would these tired, disheartened sheep find the power they needed to live a life of purpose and strength, and one day make it to their eternal home. As a result, He was compelled to keep pressing forward . . . all the way to the cross.

I believe God allowed me to see the mountain people of northern India this same way—from His perspective. When I observed the evening fires being lit that December day in 1971, I didn't just envision hundreds of families preparing their evening meals. I was moved with compassion for the thousands of individuals who were lost and without hope. I visualized countless souls, passing into eternity, having never heard the truth.

I heard God's very heartbeat for all who warranted at least one chance during their lifetime to hear the Christmas story.

From that moment on, the love of Christ constrained me. I could no longer live for myself. As 2 Corinthians 5:14–15 says, *For the love of Christ compels us…and He died for all, that those who live should live no longer for themselves, but for Him who died for them and rose again* (NKJV).

How about you? Are you moved with compassion for the people you meet and deal with each day? Does the love of Jesus compel you to live for Him and to share His amazing story? If not, ask God to help you to look past the surface and see individuals as He sees them. Once you understand their desperate need for Jesus, sowing seeds of His mercy and love won't be an occasional event for you—it will become your way of life.

And remember, you don't need to wait until Christmas to share the Savior's story; you can start today. Anytime is a great time to tell someone of His love!

> *Father, open my eyes to the needs around me each day. Give me a heart to see people as You see them. Fill me with compassion for the lost, that I might be compelled to reach out to them with the love of Christ. Create in them a hunger to know You, and prepare their hearts to receive the truth. Then, no matter the time of year, give me the opportunity to share with them the redemptive story of Jesus. These things I ask in His name. Amen.*

Chapter 2

A SECOND CHANCE AT LIFE

Yet Thou art He who didst bring me forth from the womb.
—Psalm 22:9

T HE DOOR OF THE ROOM OPENED SLOWLY, AND AN OLD MIDWIFE
peered through the crack and announced, "It's a boy!" Everyone
who had gathered outside the labor room was very happy, especially when they learned that both the mother and child were safe and
healthy. It was April 13, 1942. My mother, Ammu, had just given birth
to her second child. When my relatives saw the newborn, one of them
commented, "Why, he's as handsome as his father!" My father wasn't
there to hear the compliment. He was far from home, working as a superintendent of a rubber estate.

But all was not well with the handsome baby boy. There was a peculiar
reddish mass on his back that was obviously creating difficulties for him.

The infant had a serious birth defect we now know as spina bifida cystica, a condition in which a portion of the spinal cord protrudes through an opening of the skin on the back.

A physician came and gave medication to the infant, and at the nearby church many people prayed faithfully for the boy. But the mass was unrelenting. A few days later, the baby died.

Heartbroken, my mother sobbed bitter tears into her pillow. Her own mother tried to console her as well, but it was no use. Finally, in exasperation, my grandmother exclaimed, "Daughter, at this rate you will die of grief!"

My mother's older brother made arrangements for the funeral. The baby couldn't be buried in the church cemetery because he hadn't been baptized, so a small grave was dug in the corner of the family property. Meanwhile, someone went to inform my father of his son's death, even though the funeral could not be postponed until his return.

Back at home, Ammu was inconsolable as she listened to the sound of men digging her son's grave. She glanced helplessly at the limp body of her beloved baby boy and prayed as only a brokenhearted mother can pray.

All at once, something caught her eye. For an instant, she thought the baby had moved his fingers. Ammu stared at them with earnest intensity. Could it be true? Yes! His fingers were moving! Through tears of joy, she shouted, "Mother, he's alive! He's alive! My son is alive!"

Ammu grabbed her baby and clutched him tightly to her chest, her heart pounding with excitement. The house, which just moments before had been a house of mourning, suddenly became a house of rejoicing. The precious baby who had been dead was now alive again!

This is *my* story—an amazing story of birth, death, and a second chance at life. From death to life by the gracious hand of the Lord! Instead of a funeral and burial, a joyous celebration took place as I was christened "Varghese."

PHYSICALLY WHOLE BUT SPIRITUALLY DEAD

I recovered fully and grew healthy and strong. But from the time I was a child, I was very impressionable. It was as if something drove me to emulate the bad habits of those around me. For example, if I saw someone smoking a cigarette, I would suddenly have a burning desire to smoke a cigarette. Perhaps it was the fallen nature that rages in all of us. All I knew was that I could not quench the desire to copy the destructive behavior of others.

Even after the Lord saved me and brought me into His kingdom, I struggled against the desire to emulate people. Fortunately, my redemption in the Lord created within me a desire to imitate the godly qualities in others as well, and thereby to heed Paul's admonition in Ephesians 5:1 to *be imitators of God, as beloved children.*

My parents were devout members of the Orthodox Syrian Church (which is much like the Catholic Church), and endeavored to instill godly qualities in me from my earliest childhood. My mother was a kindhearted woman who often denied herself for the sake of her children. If there wasn't enough food to go around, she did without. She taught us from the book of Proverbs, instilling its pearls of wisdom into our tender spirits.

I took pride in my father who used to tell us, "Children, no evil shall befall you because I have not harmed the poor, defenseless, or orphans; nor have their tears fallen at my gate."

My father was the third of four sons whose family lived a hand-to-mouth existence. The meager income his family earned from the land they worked was barely enough to support them. His mother (my grandmother) was a deeply devout woman from a well-respected evangelical church family. She woke up early every morning, recited her favorite psalm, and then prayed for each of her children. She taught her children self-respect, and hoped and prayed for deliverance from the cycle of poverty. Her prayers rang in my father's ears, and at a young age, he resolved to do whatever it took to remove the tears from his mother's eyes.

At one point, someone suggested to my father that he should buy peanuts, roast them, and then sell them in the marketplace. He took that advice and went out that same day, but because selling in the marketplace was considered to be the responsibility of the poorest of poor boys and girls, he was ashamed to be seen in the market. So he prayed that he wouldn't run into anyone he knew. As he approached the marketplace, he saw one of his classmates coming toward him. Too embarrassed to face his friend, my father ran and hid under a bush. With his face pressed to the ground, he blurted out a prayer, saying, "God, I am so ashamed to beg! Please provide me a job with enough income to meet my daily needs."

Even during days of severe hunger, my grandmother told him of the great God of the Bible who blesses His children, and my father believed in that God. Because he was an industrious young man, he eventually bought a small she-goat. He carefully nurtured the goat, often taking her with him to school and tying her outside the classroom so that she could graze. During the break between classes, he would move the goat to another spot with fresh grass for munching.

Over time, his diligent care paid off. When the goat gave birth to a few kids, my father had a regular income. Years later, when he talked to us about those days, he proudly told us that the other children wore only a mundu, a skirt that covered the body from waist to ankle; however, in addition to owning a mundu, he was able to buy a shawl to cover his chest, which was the sign of wealth and dignity. He wanted us to know that he dressed like a gentleman even during his school days.

My father eventually joined an English school in order to become a government employee. Around that time, he took the advice of a friend who encouraged him to start a chitfund. A chitfund is a private savings fund, involving the participation of approximately forty people, with each one depositing a specified amount into the fund. Every month, one member is chosen by lot to receive the money that was collected that month. In due time, each participant receives a set amount from the fund. Because my father was faithful in all his dealings, he was able to build the chitfund into a fairly large sum. But because he spent so much time working the fund, he began to neglect his studies.

At one point he borrowed some money from the fund to help with the expenses of his younger sister's marriage. When he was unable to pay the money back, he ran away, eventually finding a job on a rubber estate. He worked the estate faithfully and sent home whatever he could save to help provide for his family. To supplement his income, at night he took on a second job, pressing rubber sheets.

Because of his commitment to support his parents and younger brothers and sisters, he put off marrying until he was thirty years old. When he finally married, he and my mother had two children—me and my older sister, Lilly, who later passed away when she was ten years old. Just before she died, my father lost his job and was unable to continue sending money home to his parents. When he returned home, he was shocked by how rudely he was treated by the family he had worked so hard to help support. In addition to losing his job and income, he had lost the respect of his family. It seemed that everything he had worked so hard for had evaporated.

Leaving his wife and two children at home, my father set out to find a job, ultimately landing one as the superintendent of another rubber estate. My mother joined him a short while later, and the two of them worked very hard to cultivate the estate. They raised cows and grew crops on the wetlands they had leased.

My industrious father began to organize new chitfunds and to save his money. He eventually bought more than three acres of land and built a house on it. Soon after, he bought another plot of land near the first estate and built another house. He also bought a car, and later another one. All of his daughters were eventually given in marriage, and in keeping with Indian tradition, he provided the appropriate dowries. And finally, he was always kind to the poor because he never forgot the poverty of his youth.

My father's position of authority afforded him numerous opportunities to make money through dishonest gain. But his fear of God kept him on the road of integrity. A devout member of the Jacobite Syrian Orthodox Church, he was honored by everyone in the surrounding villages as a fair and honest man.

I remember many people coming to our door with bribes, hoping that their offers of financial gain would influence my father to hire them. But the inducements didn't work. Father always declined the bribes, heeding instead the admonition of 1 Thessalonians 5:22 to *abstain from every form of evil.*

My father walked three miles through hills and valleys every Sunday to attend church, setting an uncompromising example for his children. Never was his faith shaken—not when my older sister died, not when I dropped out of school, nor when my younger brother's spinal cord was severed in a terrible bus accident. At times like these, Father would disappear into the solitude of the rubber estate and pour his heart out to God, beating his chest and quoting the scriptures of blessing that God had poured out on Abraham, Isaac, and Jacob.

My father shunned black magic and witchcraft practices, which were ingrained in our culture and were often used to harm others. However, he did occasionally consult astrologers to have them cast off evil spells, since the Jacobite Church hadn't yet started teaching that this ritual was patently wrong.

Father used to invite evangelists to our home, and he prayed with them and even helped them financially. I am convinced that God saw my father's heart, and for that reason stretched out the welcoming arm of salvation to him. Although he practiced Christian principles, my father was, as 2 Timothy 3:5 says, "holding to a form of godliness, but denying its power." He knew the Bible stories and told them to us often, but he did not know the doctrine. So even though he had always been a man who lived by strict moral principles, it would be several years later before he would experience the life-changing power of being born again.

After I got saved, whenever I would try to share the gospel with him, he would dodge the issue of his own need for God by talking about the faith of his forefathers. Finally when he could no longer resist the grace of God, he accepted Jesus Christ as his personal Lord and Savior. Three days later, he was baptized. Not long after that, my mother also gave her heart and life to the Lord.

I remember an incident that occurred in 1984. I had come home exhausted from an evangelical meeting where I had been speaking, and I was hoping to be able to sleep late the next morning. I knew that my father would be up singing before the dawn, as was his custom, and that he would expect me to sing and pray with him.

That night he asked my mother when supper would be ready. It was still light outside, but he was tired and wanted to go to bed. This was highly unusual because he never went to bed early. Even after he retired, he would stay up late, talking with my mother about various issues and the practical matters of the household.

I also went to sleep early that night, and when I awoke the next morning, it was after six o'clock. There was no sound of singing or prayer coming from my father's room. I peered in and was surprised to find him sound asleep, so I woke him up and asked if everything was okay.

"Son," he answered, "ever since I received my salvation, I have known great peace. From that first day, I have slept peacefully all night long and awakened refreshed. It is a blessing that came to me after I was saved. You led me into this salvation experience, and for that, I praise God!"

It thrilled my heart to hear him speak those words. He spent his last years praying, sharing the testimony of God's transforming love, and doing the work of the Lord in his own humble way. He prayed often and always had enough money to meet his basic needs and still give to the Lord's work. My father lived a righteous life and peacefully slept in the Lord, a rich man. It is a privilege for me to be called his son.

I remember another incident that might shed more light on his penitent character. He once asked me if I knew why we hadn't stayed in the first house he had built on the three acres of estate land he had purchased. I sat close to him and listened carefully as he explained. "You were young then," he began. "I wanted to build a nice house, so I saved some money and borrowed the rest in order to get the house built. But I only paid for part of the wood that was needed. The rest of it was stolen from the forest. The carpenters made the rafters and crossbeams from the stolen wood, and I went with them and helped bring it home in bullock-carts."

He took a deep breath and continued. "When the house was finished, we had a house-warming party. After everyone left, I asked for a lamp to be lit and brought into the drawing room, where I was relaxing in a comfortable chair. We had just moved in and didn't have a lamp with us, so your mother lit a candle and placed it on the cloth-covered table. I dozed off for a bit, and when I awoke, there were flames coming from the table! Your sister had knocked the candle over, and the tablecloth had caught fire. When I yelled for help, everyone came running in and helped us put out the fire.

"In those days, I believed in omens and premonitions, and to me, that fire was a bad omen. From my chair, I cried out, 'Oh God!' When I looked up, my eyes fell on the beams made from the stolen wood, and I asked myself, 'Are you going to spend your retirement living under a roof made of stolen wood?' That day I decided to build another house. Although I stayed in that house for several more months, I had no peace there. Those were long days of agony and tears, but God gave me both a new life and a new house! Blessed be His name."

After hearing that story, I asked the Lord to make it possible for my children to be as proud of me one day as I was of my father.

Searching for the Truth

When I was a boy, my father used to tell me stories of Abraham, Isaac, and Jacob. He and my mother also introduced me to the book of Proverbs. My concept of God was limited to what I read in the Old Testament. I feared God and wanted to please Him so that He would bless me. Although our Jacobite church was three miles from home, I attended Sunday school every week. My father would give me a small offering to enable me to attend the boy's congregation in the afternoon. I took Holy Communion once a month.

When my father taught me about the boy Samuel, I was filled with a desire to minister in the church, hoping that I, too, would hear God's voice. I wanted to please God, so I decided to become a priest. When the parish priest and the rest of my family heard about my desire, they were thrilled.

At age eleven, I became an acolyte and was given a long white robe to wear when serving at the altar. I longed to meet God and hear His voice, and I was so happy that first day! Unfortunately, it didn't take long for disappointment to set in. Instead of finding God, I found an angry priest and a few ungodly ministers, much like the sons of Eli in the days of Samuel. Worship, like everything else in the service, seemed to be for the people rather than for God. Soon I became disillusioned with religion, and my hope of meeting God grew dim.

I stole money from the church and wondered why God didn't punish me. I stole grapes meant for preparing the communion wine, and again wondered why God didn't punish me or the ungodly ministers. I committed many other acts against my conscience, with no apparent repercussions. Eventually I became convinced that if there was a God, He wasn't anywhere near that church.

When I was in high school, a Hindu teacher told me that there was a void in the heart of every person and the void could be filled through yoga. I certainly felt that void, so I eagerly began practicing the art. It didn't take me long to discover that God doesn't commune with man through yoga. Although it may be good for the body, I learned that yoga was nothing more than a waste of my time in my search for God. So I soon gave yoga up.

After high school, I joined a polytechnic institute, and as a result, I had to live away from home. I enjoyed my newfound freedom and began to dabble in all sorts of sin. I took up smoking, learned palmistry and hypnotism, and excelled at being a hypocrite. I played cards all night and slept all day. Gradually my sinful lifestyle consumed me, and I lost interest in my studies.

Even so, a great fear haunted me. Deep within, I desperately wanted to please my parents and to be a good person. But no matter how hard I tried, I continued to be a slave to my bad habits.

Hoping that I would return home a changed person, in April 1960, my mother persuaded me to attend the All Kerala Christian Fellowship. She introduced me to some of the young people there, and I began attending their prayer meetings. During one particular meeting, several of those who were filled with the Holy Spirit began to pray in the Spirit out loud. As they did, an overwhelming sense of conviction came over me, and I cried out to God. I then went home and fell at my mother's feet, begging her forgiveness for my previous behavior. But the change didn't last long. As soon as I returned to the institute, all my bad habits came flooding back, and I eventually stopped going to class altogether.

Needless to say, I failed the next year. Realizing that I knew nothing about the subjects I was supposed to be studying, in shame and desperation I borrowed money in my father's name and ran away.

I was as far away from God as it was possible to be, and I had no idea how to bridge the gap.

ON THE JOURNEY TOWARD TRUE LIFE

I faced numerous issues on my journey to find true life through Jesus Christ. See if you recognize any similar struggles in your own life:

- You attend church but have never met Jesus Christ personally.
- You've repented of sin and asked God for forgiveness, but have seen no lasting change.

- You've known God in the past but are running from Him today.
- You wrestle fear often and always end up defeated.
- You work hard and achieve significant goals, but have no inner peace.
- You attempt to please people but seem to fall short time and again.
- You are enslaved to bad habits.

Today, if you see any patterns like these in yourself, know that you're not alone. None of us are immune to sin, and we all fight our flesh and the enemy of our soul, the devil. The good news is, when Jesus shed His blood, He paid the price for every struggle we would ever encounter.

If you have never received Him as your Savior and made Him Lord over every area of your life, your victory is as close as a submitted will. His desire is that you would live life to the fullest. Don't put off receiving Him and making Him your Lord another moment!

If you *have* received Jesus, but you're still struggling with sin or running in the opposite direction from God today, why not surrender every area of your life to Him right now? He loves you and will help you overcome as you lean on Him and trust Him completely.

> *Father, I come to you in Jesus' name and by His blood, thanking You for the price Jesus paid for me so that I could know You and walk in freedom. I repent of sin. Forgive me for _____ (name any sin you need to repent of). Jesus, cleanse me and come into my life. I confess You as my Lord and Savior, and believe that God raised You from the dead. Now, according to Romans 10:9–10, I am saved!*
>
> *Holy Spirit, I welcome You into my heart and life. Fill every part of me. Right now, I surrender to You the area(s) of _____ (name any area of*

struggle that you need to surrender), and I ask that You would quicken me with Your resurrection power, according to Romans 8:11.

Jesus, I recognize that apart from You, I can do nothing, but that with You, I have victory over sin and freedom from all bondage. Thank You for Your strength and grace! In Your name I pray. Amen.

Chapter 3

A Winding Journey to Adulthood

"'For I know the plans that I have for you,' declares the Lord, 'plans
for welfare and not for calamity to give you a future and a hope.'"
—Jeremiah 29:11

WITH THE MONEY I HAD "BORROWED," I TRAVELED ACROSS North Kerala. There I found my way to the office of a Malayalam newspaper. Since I needed a job, I lied to the newspaper's owner, telling him that I wasn't able to continue my studies because of my parents' untimely deaths. He felt sorry for me and gave me a job. I worked there for six months, until I was caught red-handed stealing newspapers from the press. Naturally, I was fired on the spot.

With no job and no income, I was reduced to sleeping among the destitute in the railway stations. Eventually my uncle found me and took me home.

ADVENTURES IN THE MILITARY AND THE ROMAN CATHOLIC CHURCH

Back home again, I continued to let sin reign in my life, and my bad habits became a burden for my parents. I was disrespectful and rebelled against their discipline. One day my mother scolded me for something, and I gave a smart-alecky reply and turned to walk away. She grabbed my shirt, and when I pulled away, it tore. With uncontrollable anger, I ripped it off, threw it in her face, and stormed off.

My father nearly cursed me when he heard about my horrendous behavior. So I promptly ran away to Bombay, where I joined the military and served as a clerk.

In those new surroundings, I managed to develop even more bad habits. I smoked constantly, puffing away nearly five packs a day! To save money, I bought tobacco and paper and rolled my own cigarettes, but it didn't make a dent in my consumption. I puffed away on one as I rolled another.

I also began drinking heavily, eventually finding it necessary to add two shots of rum to my morning tea. Alcohol became my constant companion. When I ran short of money to support my habits, I resorted to illegal activities to supplement my income.

I had become a slave to the sins that had seemed so appealing to me in the beginning. Now there was an aching emptiness in my soul, and I knew that I needed to change my life. So I visited several temples, vainly searching for the answer to my gnawing discontent.

A Roman Catholic priest told me that I could find the peace I was seeking through their church if I would embrace "the true church founded by the apostle Peter." So I joined the church, confessed my sins, prayed their prayers, recited the Nicene Creed, and said Hail Marys. But the cigarettes in my pocket and the rum in my hand reared their ugly heads and mocked me. Feeling utterly hopeless, I developed an aversion to Christian institutions. It would be a while before I learned the truth of Ephesians 2:8–9: *For by grace you have been saved through faith; and that not of yourselves, it is the gift of God; not as a result of works, that no one should boast.*

Disillusioned, I began to take my cues from some local atheists and started speaking against the church and disturbing prayer meetings. With a Bible in one hand and a glass of whiskey in the other, I angrily "preached" against Jesus.

Driven by my need to find an answer for my miserable state, I even went to the Hindu temples and asked the devils for a touch of black magic. I wanted to experience supernatural power. I tried everything to get the spirits to come into me and possess me, but they never came. I know now that God, in His mercy, protected me.

But sin's dark hold was unrelenting. A few months later I was transferred to Delhi, where I learned to write false accounts in the military canteen and also devised other ways to steal money. Needless to say, my life was as hollow as a discarded locust shell.

On Christmas Day in 1968, I was overcome by a desire to turn over a new leaf. I went to a Roman Catholic church near Delhi, where the relics of the apostle Thomas are said to be buried. Thousands of people gather there every year for the Christmas service that's conducted in a tent outside the church. I bought a ticket, which allowed me the privilege of sitting on a chair, while those without a ticket sprawled on the floor.

Expecting nothing, I ventured into the dimly lit church. Standing in front of the crucifix, I burst into tears, fell prostrate on the worn, wooden floor, and begged to have the burden of my sin removed from my heart. I prayed to the apostle Thomas, to Jesus, to St. George, and to the Virgin Mary. My tears and wailing brought only a small measure of relief.

I then went back to the tent where the Christmas service was being held. Although I couldn't understand what was going on, I received communion. Suddenly a feeling of utter failure overwhelmed me. I had cried and prayed in vain. I hadn't changed at all.

Enraged and at the same time hopeless, I stormed out of the tent, jumped into the military vehicle that had been waiting for me, and returned to the barracks. I was trapped in the bondage of sin, and I knew it. From that moment forward, I became a hardened atheist and abandoned myself to a reckless, immoral life.

A DIVINE APPOINTMENT

In India, arranged marriages are the cultural norm, and despite my rebellion in every other area of my life, I had no inclination to resist the tradition. The arrangement is considered a social contract between two families as much as one between two people. Love is an important element, but is believed to evolve naturally and grow stronger during the course of a shared life.

Somehow I was content to leave it to my parents to find a suitable bride for me. Whenever I was home on leave, a number of marriage proposals were offered to my parents on my behalf. My father was selective, insisting that a prospective bride must come from a good family background and social status.

I told my mother, "I will marry any girl you approve," but I often dreamed that my future wife would be a tall and fashionable blonde beauty like the ones I had seen on movie posters!

One day a man approached my parents about considering his sister Lilly as a prospective bride. She had been unsuccessful in getting into the School of Physics. My parents and I agreed to meet Lilly, and when I saw her, I immediately noticed she had none of the seductive charms a woman usually uses to entice a man. Frankly, at first glance, I wasn't all that impressed. She later told me that she hadn't wanted to marry a soldier, so she had worn faded clothes and washed her hair with course soap so that she wouldn't appear the least bit attractive!

When we got back home, my sister asked, "How do you like the girl?"

I replied, "She looks like our maidservant's sister. She's so short that I could carry her on my shoulders."

So much for my tall, blonde beauty! But unbeknownst to me, she had been born again as a young girl.

My parents approved of Lilly, so as I had promised, I married her. Our wedding was held on July 24, 1967. Soon the Lord would prove the truth of Proverbs 18:22, that *He who finds a wife finds a good thing, and obtains favor from the* Lord. But before that truth could become reality for me, there were other issues I needed to deal with.

Despair unto Death

When Lilly and I married, I was still working at the military canteen. Eventually the false accounts I had set up were discovered, and criminal charges were filed against me. I knew there would be no escaping punishment, and I had no doubt that I would end up in jail. In the end, no matter how hard I wrestled to come up with a solution, there seemed to be only one escape—suicide.

I made up my mind once and for all to end my life, and I managed to smuggle enough sleeping pills from the army hospital to do the job. I decided to spend my last night on earth at the movie theater. Afterward, I went back to my room and wrote a few letters to my friends. Interestingly enough, although I'd been married for over two years, I didn't have the courage to write a farewell letter to my wife.

After finishing the letters, I paced the room. Then resigning myself to the task at hand, I went up to the terrace, clutching the sleeping pills in my trembling hand.

Suddenly a voice pierced the darkness, startling me. "My son, don't you believe there is a God and that heaven and hell are real?"

Despite my atheistic stance, I knew in my heart that God was real. But before I could answer, the voice continued.

"If God is a reality, and heaven and hell are realities, where will you go when you die and your spirit has to stand before God?"

The inner turmoil I felt at that moment was furious and unrelenting. If God did not exist, as my beliefs had tried to convince me, I would escape. But if God was real, I was utterly helpless and undone.

The truth is, I was afraid of hell . . . and afraid to die. My father had warned me about the fiery furnace, and the very thought of burning in hell frightened me enough to cause me to abort my suicide attempt. I flung the sleeping pills off the terrace roof and raced back to my room. Then grabbing my journal, I wrote the sentiments of my tortured heart, "I am not yet ready to die."

I had no idea how I'd follow through with it, but I made a decision then and there—from that time forward, I would face whatever consequences lay ahead and do everything I could to live a good life.

While the army's case against me was still in progress, I read the biography of Mahatma Gandhi. Gandhi was a dedicated reformer who, through nonviolent action, fought to free his fellow citizens from the chains of colonial rule. Reading his story ignited a desire within me to live for the good of my fellow man. I had not known before reading this book that the Sermon on the Mount (see Matthew 5) was Gandhi's inspiration for becoming a servant of society.

I promptly read the gospel of Matthew and resolved to volunteer for social causes.

THE MERCY AND GRACE OF GOD

By nothing less than the miraculous grace of God, the only punishment I received in the military canteen case was a transfer. Clearly, God had other plans for my life than prison.

Lilly was expecting a baby at the time, but soon afterward, she had a miscarriage, which affected us both deeply. In an effort to keep her mind off the loss and restore a measure of happiness to her life, I took her on picnics and to the movies, and did whatever else I thought might speed up the healing process.

Several months after the miscarriage, Lilly greeted me at the door when I came home from work one day. She said, "Let's go to church. Brother Jordan Khan is speaking tonight."

I suggested going to a movie instead, but I could see that she wasn't happy about it. Her heart seemed to be set on going to church. So I agreed to go with her, only relenting because she was again expecting a child and I hoped my presence might help to prevent another miscarriage.

That night, Brother Khan spoke from John 1:12: *But as many as received Him, to them He gave the right to become children of God, even to those who believe in His name.* Brother Khan explained so clearly what it means to be a true Christian that I was forced to admit to myself I had never received Jesus Christ as my personal Lord and Savior—that, in fact, I was not a Christian. My atheistic beliefs had been shattered, and I knew for certain that God was real. But I realized there was no amount of effort I could put forth in trying to be a good person that would ever be enough to please a holy God.

The next day Lilly expressed her desire to go to the meeting again, but I quickly said no. Immediately, she felt a sharp pain in her lower abdomen and had to lie down on the cot. Uncomfortable and distressed, she pleaded with me to go to the meeting without her. And again, in the hope of warding off another miscarriage, I went.

I regret to admit that I was tempted to go to a movie instead. But knowing that Lilly would ask me about Brother Khan's sermon, I decided I'd better go so that I'd be able to answer her. That night, the message was from Revelation 3:20: "'*Behold, I stand at the door and knock; if any one hears My voice and opens the door, I will come in to him, and will dine with him, and he with Me.*'" As Brother Khan spoke, I felt an overwhelming urge to accept Jesus as my Lord and Savior. But for some reason, I resisted the urge to open my heart to Him. When the meeting ended, I was irrational and angry with everyone, especially Jordan Khan, who stood at the door shaking hands and greeting people as they left. I turned and slipped out the back door to avoid having to speak with him. As soon as I walked out the door, an army officer waved me over and said, "Get in the truck, and I'll give you a lift."

Though the truck was jam-packed with other men, I managed to squeeze into the back corner where, completely dejected, I sat with my head in my hands. Then, as the truck lurched forward, a huge wave of conviction washed over me. It seemed as though every sin I had committed since childhood paraded through my mind. When I realized the sheer magnitude of my iniquity, a stream of hot tears began to spill from my eyes. A single thought cycled over and over in my tortured mind: *Who can save me from this overwhelming load of sins?*

Moments later, two Bible verses formed in my mind: "'*Behold, I stand at the door and knock; if anyone hears My voice and opens the door, I will come in*'" (Revelation 3:20), and "*I will give you a new heart*" (Ezekiel 36:26).

I was utterly brokenhearted over my sins. So one by one, I began to confess them to God. Crushed by the weight of my innumerable transgressions, I begged for the forgiveness that He alone could give.

Then all at once it happened. Suddenly a wave of peace such as I had never known before washed over me. The load of sin lifted. It was gone— and I was bathed in pure joy! I lost all sense of time as the love of God enveloped me.

The next thing I knew, someone was shaking me awake. The truck was empty. I jumped out and ran like a gazelle all the way home. If I live to be a thousand, I will never forget that night. It was October 1, 1971—in the back of a military truck—when God saw fit to save my soul from death.

I burst through the door of our house and shouted to Lilly, "God has saved me! We have had a picture of Jesus and a crucifix blessed by the Pope in our room for all this time, and they didn't save me! But tonight

Jesus came into my heart, and He saved me and set me free from the awful burden of my sins!"

Lilly began to cry.

"Why are you crying?" I asked. "I have Jesus in my heart! I am filled with joy!"

"I have Him in my heart too," she whispered.

I was shocked! "In the five years we have been married, why haven't you ever told me this before?" I asked.

"I was afraid that you would hate me. You were always running around saying you were an atheist and angrily asking God if He was real. So I kept silent and poured my heart out to the Lord, praying that you would turn to Him."

I smiled at her as I gently wiped the tears from her cheeks. "Well, my dear, your prayers have been answered!"

Unable to contain my joy, I ran to my neighbors and told them that Jesus had saved me. The next day at work, I declared to everyone I saw, "Jesus has saved me!" I was energized and filled with peace. God had given me a new hope and a fresh start.

At that moment, I never could have dreamed all that He had in store for me. All I knew was that in the back of a crowded army truck, God had reached out in His mercy and grace, and promoted a simple soldier to the higher ranks of a heavenly mission, to engage in the relentless battle against Satan's dark kingdom.

THE DIFFERENCE IN NIGHT AND DAY

The before-and-after pictures of a person who has received Jesus Christ provide a contrast as sharp as night and day. In fact, John 1:4–5 describes the difference as the literal transformation of darkness to light: *Life itself was in him, and this life gives light to everyone. The light shines through the darkness, and the darkness can never extinguish it* (NLT). Ephesians 5:8 depicts this same truth: *You were formerly darkness, but now you are light in the Lord.*

Consider the characteristics I exhibited in my former life, compared to those found in my new life in Christ:

Before	After
Empty religiousness and traditionalism	Passion to know God and share Jesus' love
Fear of man and of the unknown	Faith in God and His Word
Disrespect, rebellion, anger	Compassion for others
Dishonesty, lawlessness	Dependability, swiftness to repent
Addictive behaviors, insecurities	Peace, assurance of eternal security
Enslavement to sin	Freedom to live righteously
Hopelessness, disillusionment	Renewed hope, joy from deep within
Suicidal tendencies	Energy to live and fulfill God's purpose for my life

The distinct differences in these two lifestyles cannot be denied—and should not be dismissed! But only by receiving Jesus Christ can such life-altering exchanges be made. If this striking contrast between darkness and light compels you to turn to Him, why not ask Him to flood your life with His light ... today!

> *Father God, I come to You in Jesus' name. I am tired of walking in darkness and living my life running from You. I realize religion is not the answer for breaking the bondage*

of sin in my life, so I ask You to fill me with the light of Your presence—right now. I receive Jesus into my life, into every area and every part. My desire is to walk each day in Your light. I renounce sin. Forgive me, cleanse me, and loose me completely from the bondage that has held me in its grip. I choose light in place of darkness. Thank You, Father, for being the light of my life! In the name of Jesus, I pray. Amen.

Chapter 4

ANSWERING GOD'S CALL

He came for a witness, that he might bear witness of the light,
that all might believe through him.
—John 1:7

Two months went by, and Christmas was drawing near. It was at this time that Lilly and I went out for a walk and saw the cooking fires on the mountainside. Today I know that it was the Holy Spirit who prompted me to ask, "Shouldn't those people hear the story of Christmas at least once?"

Although I was still in the army, I became a missionary the moment I was converted. Looking for ways I could minister while still working, I sent off for gospel tracts and booklets. After the morning service on Christmas Day, I handed out tracts to the patients in the military hospital, as well as to Pakistani prisoners. When my pastor heard what I was doing, he encouraged me to continue using the tracts as witnessing tools. I needed that encouragement.

At first I was somewhat embarrassed to hand the tracts to people, so I would place them on park benches and in culverts, and watch with satisfaction when someone picked one up to read. Then one day while I was praying, I had a vision of the Lord Jesus being crucified—naked but not ashamed as His mother and other women stood by His side. Suddenly I had an overwhelming sense of His great love for me, and this question came to me: "Jesus was willing to bear the shame of the cross to save you; now will you be ashamed to proclaim His love?"

As a deep conviction washed over me, I told myself, "Never again." And from that day on I was able to share the gospel boldly, without a trace of embarrassment.

The Lord provided many opportunities for me to witness for Him. I carried tracts with me to pass out wherever I went. The minute I got off work, I walked to nearby villages, going from house to house, handing out tracts and talking to people about Jesus.

I also had a tremendous desire to tell the men in uniform about the saving grace of the Lord Jesus Christ. I witnessed everywhere I went—in the office, in the army barracks, and in the hospitals. I distributed thousands of tracts and held gospel meetings at the front gates of the military barracks. There was a rule that military personnel were not supposed to distribute tracts on government property, but I ignored the rule because my obedience to God's admonition to share His message was the higher law.

LEARNING GOD'S WAYS

The job I had at that time required me to be in the office on holidays and Sundays, which made it impossible for me to attend weekly worship services. But God faithfully provided the fellowship and spiritual growth that I needed by bringing godly people into my life to help me mature. Pastor P. M. Thomas and his wife, Christy, were one such couple. Another instrumental person was Captain A. M. Samuel, an army officer who boldly distributed tracts and visited people's homes to share the gospel. He taught me how to conduct open-air meetings and to pray for the sick. These and numerous other wonderful people taught me God's ways—both from the Bible and through the good examples they set in their daily lives.

I also learned God's ways from the Lord Himself. In fact, He taught me things that no one else could teach me. After I was saved, the first thing He instructed me to do was to clean up my house. Though the liquor and cigarettes were long gone, I still needed to throw out all the movie star pictures that decorated my walls and get rid of the playing cards that had dominated my spare time.

I began to pray every day, both in the morning and the evening. I didn't have a Bible, so I bought two—one in my native language and one in English. Hungry to learn more, I began to study the Bibles earnestly. I also started reading good Christian books and magazines, making sure that I always had something on hand to read at the bus stop or during my lunch break.

As I read my Bible and prayed, the Lord began to teach me how to walk in obedience to His Word.

STEPS OF OBEDIENCE

The first time I saw adult believers being baptized, I was amazed. Prior to that, I had only been familiar with infant baptism as practiced by the Jacobite Church. However, I was touched by the confession of these people and struck by the similarity of their baptism to the baptism of Jesus.

A few days later as I was hurrying to my office, I heard a voice whisper, "You should be baptized." I was somewhat amused because I had been baptized when I was three months old. It didn't make sense to me to be baptized again.

But one day as I reflected on the baptisms I had witnessed, I became convinced that it was God who had spoken to me. When I went home for lunch that day, I announced to Lilly that I was going to be baptized. To my surprise, she became quite angry and accused me of being unduly influenced by the Pentecostals or Brethren pastors.

I tried to explain what had happened, but she kept arguing that the Pentecostals and Brethren baptized even those who had been raised in Christian homes, regardless of whether or not they had already been baptized as infants. She insisted that a second baptism wasn't necessary, and she offered to give me a book on the subject written by an Episcopal priest. Since my Bible knowledge was still quite limited, I was confused about what to do.

Finally I said, "Lilly, let's pray. We will obey what God tells us to do." I knelt down and prayed, "God, I don't know whether I should be baptized again or not. Speak to us as we look in Your Word."

I pulled out the small New Testament that I always kept in my pocket, opened it, and read Acts 2:37–47. I glanced back at verse 41, which was underlined in my *Soul Winner's Bible,* and read out loud, *Then those who gladly received His word were baptized* (NKJV). I turned to my wife and said, "I received the salvation of God on October 1, but I wasn't baptized. Now that He has confirmed it through His Word, I want to be baptized. I don't care what the minister of our church or anyone else thinks."

"You can get baptized if you want, but please don't insist that I do it too," Lilly snapped.

"No," I replied, "I won't try to persuade you. You should only do it if you decide for yourself that you should."

I was told that the pastor of our church wouldn't perform the baptism, so I wrote to my uncle who agreed with my decision. He said he would make arrangements to baptize me when I came to Kerala to visit my family during vacation.

In the meantime, I decided to share my thoughts with the pastor of the local church. He asked why I wanted to be baptized, and I told him how the Lord had spoken to me and confirmed it when I asked Him what I should do. He agreed that it was a good thing, and then he said, "My wife and I were baptized recently. When winter is over, I will baptize you."

Lilly was nearing the end of her pregnancy, and I wanted to consecrate the child to God. So I told the pastor, and we set the date to consecrate the baby immediately after I was baptized. A week before the service, Lilly came to me and said, "Next week we are going to be baptized, right?"

Her question confused me. "What do you mean 'we'?" I asked. "Whose baptism are you talking about?"

"Ours," she replied with a shy smile. "I knew from the very beginning that it was the right thing to do, but I was afraid of offending my older brother and the other church members. But how can I stay behind when you are going ahead? I am coming with you!"

So on March 12, Lilly and I were baptized, and our son Aby was consecrated to the Lord. It was a beautiful, joy-filled day, and we sensed the overwhelming presence of the Lord in our hearts. It was an especially sweet day too, because after Lilly's miscarriage, the doctors had told us she would never bear children. But our God is a God of the impossible. He had given us a healthy son, the first of our five children, and with overflowing gladness, we presented him to God, praying that he would become a servant of the Lord.

The day of our baptism was an unforgettable experience. Whenever I reminisce about it now, I find myself wishing I could be baptized all over again!

COAL AND A SOUL

A few months later I was enjoying my morning meal before leaving for the office when, all at once, an inner voice interrupted my thoughts. The voice asked a simple, penetrating question: "Did you do anything for the Lord before eating your breakfast?"

Upon hearing these words, I was immediately reminded of a similar question my father had posed years earlier as I was eating breakfast one morning. "Son, have you done any work to earn your meal? It's good to ask yourself this question before you sit down to eat."

So that day, with both questions fresh on my mind, I resolved that I would only eat after I had first worked for the Lord. At the time, I could do little more than distribute tracts . . . however, I did begin handing them out before I ate breakfast!

Another time, the Lord taught me quite a memorable lesson—to share the gospel with others even when it seemed inconvenient. It was winter, and we burned coal to keep our room warm. I was on leave so that I could help Lilly, who by this time was expecting our second child. One day, I had made lunch and was in a rush to get to the military store, hoping to buy the coal we needed before the store closed. My uniform allowed me to ride in any of the military vehicles, but as I stood at the bus stop trying to flag one down, not one of them would stop.

I prayed, "Lord, You know that I have to get to the store before noon, because if I don't, we won't have enough coal to keep the room warm, and Aby will be crying all night long. So please help me."

God answered, "Share the gospel with the people standing at this bus stop."

Apparently God didn't comprehend that I was in a big hurry. There was no time to witness to these people and get to the store before it closed. I quickly handed tracts to the people around me, and resumed waving frantically at the passing trucks. Still, no one would stop.

When I reminded the Lord of my time constraints, He replied, "I asked you to share the gospel, not hand out tracts."

As I was standing there deciding what to do, two soldiers came to me with tracts in their hands and asked me what they were. "We can't understand any of this," they said.

"They contain some of the words of Jesus," I explained as I anxiously looked for the next military vehicle.

One of the soldiers asked, "Could you please tell us some of His teachings?"

In those days I could only speak fluently in Malayalam. But I knew a few words of English and some Hindi, so I tried to translate Hebrews 13:5 from English into Hindi. For the words *"I will never desert you, nor will I ever forsake you,"* I somehow I managed to communicate, "Jesus said He would not leave you, but hold you."

One of the soldiers was deeply touched and said he would like to have a God who would hold him.

"God hears prayers," I explained. "He told me to share the gospel with you, and that's why I haven't been able to get a truck. Now that I have told you about Jesus, I will be able to get one and buy the coal I need."

Before I had completed the sentence, a truck sped toward us. I waved my hand and the driver stopped. "Hurry up!" he shouted. "We have to get to the military store to get coal, and we only have fifteen minutes!"

The soldiers at the bus stop could hardly believe their eyes . . . or their ears! The Lord had sent me men in a special truck—far from the main road—and the men were going to the military store to buy coal, just like I was!

When I got to the store, an officer asked, "Why did you come all this way? You could have called or sent someone. There's a sack of top-grade coal over there that I packed for our commanding officer. It's ready to go, so you might as well take it. I'll pack another sack for him."

As I left, I rejoiced over God's faithfulness. Because of my obedience in preaching His gospel to the two soldiers, God met my need by providing top-grade coal! What I didn't know at the moment was, God was about to welcome the young man I'd just witnessed to into His loving arms— for the very next day the soldier who needed a God who would hold him accepted the Lord as his Savior!

COMPLETE SURRENDER

I knew I could go more places and reach more people if I were not serving in the army. I loved sharing the gospel, and people were always captivated as they listened. But I had not yet received the call for full-time ministry. Consumed by an overwhelming desire to share the good news of Christ with others, I cried out, "Oh Lord, I know You haven't called me to work for You full time, but I'm asking You to please give me a special calling, and until then, I will only eat the midday meal."

Whether I was in the barracks or at home, I honored my pledge. At times, it was tempting to eat the evening meal instead of lunch because meat and eggs were served in the evening. But I held to my commitment.

On New Year's Day 1972, Lilly and I read the first chapter of Joshua. When we got to the sixteenth verse, we read together, *"All that you have commanded us we will do, and wherever you send us we will go."*

There was a special meeting at church that evening, and to our surprise, the pastor preached on the same verse we had read just hours earlier. When he asked how many would obey this verse without question, Lilly and I jumped to our feet.

In an emotional surrender of our lives, we prayed with the pastor as he said, "Lord, we will obey without question *whatever* You command us, and we will go without question *wherever* you send us." From that point on, we had a burning desire to go into full-time ministry.

"THEREFORE DO NOT FEAR . . ."

Shortly after that church meeting, God richly blessed me and gave me a special calling to preach the gospel. I am indebted to Him for His preaching grace as much as for His saving grace.

One day I received a letter from a Christian organization that addressed me as "Brother Vargis." With great excitement, I showed it to Lilly. It was as if I had been awarded a doctoral degree! I still rejoice when I am addressed as "Brother."

I sent out several applications, seeking a church group to be affiliated with, but none replied. Soon, I grew discouraged. So I shared my heart with my pastor, who advised me to remain an independent preacher. He pointed out that, as an independent, I would be able to serve God's people regardless of their denomination. He also pointed out that we wouldn't be limited by the rules and regulations of the various Christian organizations. Lilly and I were greatly encouraged by this advice.

I also wrote to several missionary organizations, but none of them offered any advice or help. Eventually the coordinator of Operation Mobilisation wrote to me saying, "If you are sure that God has called you into full-time ministry, resign your job and wait for the Lord to do a miracle. That is faith."

I was encouraged by his letter, but I wondered how our needs would be met. After all, I had a wife and a growing family to support. As I prayed, the Lord prompted me to open my Bible to Matthew 14:16–20, where I read the following:

> But Jesus said to them, "They do not need to go away; you give them something to eat!" And they said to Him, "We have here only five loaves and two fish." And He said, "Bring them here to Me." And ordering the multitudes to recline on the grass, He took the five loaves and the two fish, and looking up toward heaven, He blessed the food, and breaking the loaves He gave to the disciples, and the disciples gave them to the multitudes, and they all ate, and were satisfied. And they picked up what was left over of the broken pieces, twelve full baskets. And there were about five thousand men who ate, aside from women and children.

When I had finished reading the passage, the Lord instructed me to get a pencil and paper. I obeyed, and He asked me, "How many loaves of bread did it take to feed the five thousand?" I knew the answer was five, so I answered that question easily. But then He asked, "How many pieces of bread do you and your family need each day?"

I quickly scribbled down some figures and came up with an answer.

Then He asked, "And how many pieces of bread do you need for a year?"

I scratched out the calculation, taking into account that Lilly and I fasted one day a week, and wrote down that number.

Then the Lord spoke to my heart and said, "I fed five thousand people with only five loaves of bread. How many loaves do I need to provide for your family for an entire year?"

Now He had my attention. It required additional calculations and estimates of how many pieces of bread are in loaf, but after I did the math, I figured that with the same "bread-stretching" process God had used to feed the five thousand, it would take less than a loaf and a half!

I lifted up my eyes and stared at the wall. "How difficult is it," I asked myself, "for the God who created the universe by the power of His word to provide less than two loaves of bread for my family each year?" I knelt before the Lord, confessed my unbelief, and resolved to trust Him.

However, the next day, doubt rose up in my heart again. *Who will support me financially?* I wondered. I applied for a day of casual leave and spent the time in prayer. The Lord dealt with me gently, saying, "When the apostle Thomas came to India, who sent him the money he needed to live? Thomas was a man of little faith. If he could come evangelize India, why can't you go in faith?" The words pierced my heart and brought to mind Hebrews 13:8: *Jesus Christ is the same yesterday and today, yes and forever.* Finally I realized that the same God who had helped Thomas in days past would help me.

Jehovah Jireh Is Faithful

During those days before I was released from the army, the Lord opened my eyes to certain mysteries of the Bible. As I sat in the His presence, He taught me from various passages of scripture as I meditated on them. The knowledge I received in these special times with God was invaluable later when I began preaching sermons.

At one point I read an article about tithing, which echoed a message our pastor had preached from Matthew 23:23. This verse pertains to the scribes and Pharisees who had tithed everything to God, including their mint and cumin, but sadly, forgot about justice and mercy. Our pastor had exhorted us to pay our tenth, and more if possible.

I was worried about tithing, and with good reason. For a long time before I was saved, we had used corrupt earnings to buy food and kerosene. After I'd given my life to the Lord, I gave up all the dishonest practices, which meant I had to buy everything legitimately—on my income alone. So it seemed like it would be too difficult to pay my tithe on top of everything else.

Nonetheless, I decided to give God 11 percent of my income. When I got my paycheck, I carefully set aside the allotted amount for the needy people and other deserving causes. I was sure that life was going to be very hard!

The next day when I went to the military store, the head clerk looked at me and asked, "Why do you go to the trouble to come here yourself? Why don't you send your assistant?"

"I can choose what I want if I come myself," I answered.

A friend standing nearby overheard our conversation and said, "I'll give you my rice quota every month for half of what you pay here. We don't eat rice."

One of the other clerks, also my friend, spoke up and said, "I can do the same with flour."

He had hardly finished speaking when an officer I had helped in the past chimed in and said, "If you'd like, I can send you the high-quality meat and vegetables I get from the officer's store."

All of this happened the same day that I determined to honor God with my tithe.

Then to top it off, my monthly expenses decreased.

These occurrences did not happen by chance—God was honoring His promise found in Malachi 3:10: *"Bring the whole tithe into the storehouse, so that there may be food in My house, and test Me now in this," says the*

LORD of hosts, *"if I will not open for you the windows of heaven, and pour out for you a blessing until there is no more need."*

Later—even during times of deprivation—we never stopped or reduced our giving to God. In turn, He gave us more and more in abundance, and we were able to increase our giving . . . and to this day, we continue to do so.

There were times when we were in great need of money, and during those seasons, we increased our giving and asked God to meet our need. Because His promises are true and He is a debtor to no man, He has always given us more than we asked for.

CLEAN HANDS AND A PURE HEART

One day I was typing a letter to Lilly in my army office when my commanding officer walked in, saw what I was doing, and asked me, "Are you typing a personal letter during office hours?" When I told him that I had finished all my work, he quickly found more for me to do.

A few days later the same thing happened again. "Preacher, are you at it again?" he asked.

"I've finished all my work," I replied. He checked my desk and saw that I was telling the truth. Then, looking at the paper in the typewriter, he asked, "Whose paper is that, preacher? Are you stealing the government's paper for personal use?"

I tried to explain myself, saying, "It's just one piece of paper. It's not stealing."

"Oh, like all preachers, you've learned to justify yourself," he spat as he walked out of the room.

Immediately the Spirit of God convicted me, and I became very upset. *I used a sheet of paper. Another man takes a fan. What's the difference?*

Though I wrestled with these thoughts for a few moments, I quickly came to grips with the truth—one item may seem small and the other large, but taking either one is stealing.

I determined then and there that I would never again steal even the smallest thing. I went to the officer's cabin, begged his forgiveness, and thanked him for showing me that I was wrong. That experience taught me the importance of having clean hands and a pure heart. Something that seemingly insignificant is significant enough to hamper our spiritual growth and damage our Christian witness.

IN THE TWINKLING OF AN EYE

I was in the habit of carrying gospel tracts in different languages so that I could distribute them to the various people who came to the office where I worked. On any given day, about three hundred officers and an equal number of soldiers came through our offices. I gave out tracts to all of them, along with the gospel of John.

One day when I was returning from the office rather late, an officer with a higher rank than mine was on duty at the gate. He had been promoted, and now I was supposed to salute him, but I was reluctant to do so because he used to salute *me* and call me "sir."

He was a military carpenter who had been promoted along with many others who had served during the Indo-Pak War in 1971. He ducked into his room when he saw me approaching, and I walked quickly by. However, the Spirit of God spoke to me, saying, "Go to that man and share the gospel."

Initially, my pride made me reluctant to approach him because I didn't want to have to salute him—but I knew I had to obey God. So I marched right into the room, gave a smart salute, and wasted no time in telling him about the changes Jesus had made in my life. He was astonished.

"If you will put your trust in Jesus and receive Him as your Lord and Savior, He will transform you and give you peace," I explained.

"I'll think about it, Vargis," he said as I handed him a tract entitled "Danger in Delay."

"Please sir," I pleaded with him, "read this before you go to sleep tonight and make a decision to make Jesus your Lord and Savior."

He agreed to read the tract, and I went home.

The next day an officer told me that the man I had pleaded with the night before was dead. "He drank some liquor, ate supper, lit the coal fire to heat his room, and went to sleep. Apparently smoke filled the room, and because his doors and windows were closed, he suffocated."

I couldn't believe my ears. The man who had heard the salvation message and taken the tract to read, set the tract on his table that night, drank some alcohol, and died. I could only trust God with his soul, but I was grateful my conscience was clear because I had obeyed the Lord's voice.

From this experience, the Holy Spirit taught me that I must obey Him immediately—and not postpone the task until tomorrow—especially when He tells me to share the gospel with someone. We never know how close a person is to eternity; he could be taken in the twinkling of an eye. Oh how important it is to be sensitive and obedient to the voice of Lord.

To Know Him

Are you compelled to know God intimately? To understand His ways? To hear His voice and be quick to obey? If so, then consider setting aside a special time each day just to be with Him—a time to read and study His Word, to worship, to pray, and to wait in His presence to hear His voice. The following suggestions may serve in helping you to get started:

- Invest in a good Bible with a concordance. There are many translations on the market today, but the best translation is the one you will actually read! You may want to consider a version that includes a daily Bible-reading/study plan. Other versions are pre-divided into daily readings so that you can cover the entire Bible in one year.

- Designate at least ten to fifteen minutes each day just for God. You may want to get up each morning a little earlier than normal so that you can give God the first moments of your day.

- Find a quiet place where you can be alone and uninterrupted. This might be a certain room in your house or a special area outside where you can focus solely on the Lord. Turn off any electronics that might distract you, such as your television, computer, and phone. Of course, you may want to play a worship CD or use a Bible software program on your computer.

- Quiet your mind and spirit. Bind the enemy, in Jesus' name. Plead the blood of Jesus over your life. Read a psalm or another passage to the Lord as you enter His presence with praise.

- In a journal or notebook, record any scriptures that stand out to you and anything you believe God is saying directly to you. You can worship and pour out your heart to Him as you write. Journaling will give you a record of how the Lord is at work in your life and will enable you to see His faithfulness in answering your requests.

- Be still before Him. Listen for His voice.

Jesus said that His sheep would hear His voice and follow Him, and they would not follow the voice of a stranger (see John 10:3–5). Recognizing His voice will become natural to you as you spend time each day in His presence—and knowing Him intimately will soon become the greatest joy of your life!

> *Father, my heart's desire is to know You, to hear Your voice and follow You. Help me to develop faithfulness as I come to You each day and open Your Word, and as I offer my praise and prayers to You. Help me to hear what the Spirit*

is saying to me and to be quick to listen and quick to obey. I realize souls are hanging in the balance, and I want to be ready! I love You, Lord, and pray these things in Your name. Amen.

Chapter 5

STEPS OF OBEDIENCE

"Go into all the world and preach the gospel to all creation."
—Mark 16:15

FROM THE MOMENT THE LORD IMPRESSED UPON MY SPIRIT THAT IT was time to quit my job and plunge into full-time gospel work, I obeyed. Looking neither to the left nor to the right, I focused only on seeking the face of the Lord.

When I prepared to hand in my initial resignation from the military, several of my officer friends advised me to withdraw the paperwork. They pleaded with me to reconsider, pointing out that I would receive a regular pension if I served for just three more years.

But I knew what the Lord had spoken to my heart. So when they brought it up again, I explained to them that I could never turn back. "When I served the government of India, I believed that it would provide for my needs. This government is volatile and unstable, but I serve an unchanging God who has promised that as I do His work, He will provide for me and my family." My chief desire was to live a true life of faith.

Just as Matthew the tax-gatherer heard and followed Jesus, I was determined to remain steadfast to the call on my life and plunge ahead into full-time ministry. All the while, I continued testifying to others about Christ, reminding them of His imminent return and the day of judgment.

My prayer was that God would send me where others were unwilling to go, and my burden was for the tribes in the border areas and in the villages along the steep Himalayan mountain switchbacks—the same people my heart went out to on that Christmas Eve in 1971.

But God spoke to me quite clearly one night, saying, "Go to Katra." This was not what I had hoped to hear. At that time, Brahmin supremacy was the core of Katra's culture, and the entire business sector was their monopoly. Katra was a place of Hindu pilgrimage, and every day thousands of people poured into the city to "sing praises to the mother." It was a giant melting pot that ensured the locals a lucrative tourist trade.*

Katra was also a land of "untouchables." Branded as such by the conservative Brahmins, these outcasts were scavengers by profession and were brutally discriminated against. Christians were considered outcasts as well, and were treated with the same disdain.

I was afraid to go to Katra. I had never been to Bible school, and at that time, I had a fairly limited knowledge of the scriptures. As doubt and fear crept in, I wondered, *How can I go and preach the gospel? How would I answer people if they asked me any questions?*

When God wouldn't let me off the hook, I knew that I had no choice but to obey Him. So I wrote a letter asking the army authorities to release me from my service. I had submitted an application a month earlier, requesting to be released so that I could take care of my aging parents.

---

*At the time of this book's publication, these points about Katra remain true.

Ordinarily, that would have been an acceptable reason for dismissal, but the request had been sent back to me without being processed.

God spoke to me about the matter. "It's true your parents are old, but you are seeking a release to preach the gospel, not to take care of your parents."

This time I wrote my testimony, and again requested a release. I told the officers that for many years I had been lost—a sinner—but now I had accepted the Lord Jesus Christ as my Savior, and had received peace. I explained that there were many who had never heard about this Savior and that I had a great desire to share the good news of Jesus Christ with them. On that basis, I asked to be released from the army so that I could evangelize India.

The officers who read my letter were amused, but each of them signed it and forwarded it to the authorities along the chain of command. When my application reached the commander of our unit, he called me into his office. A group of officers were seated there, and the commander asked me to withdraw my resignation. I firmly declined. Finally one of the officers who had constantly harassed me since my conversion said, "We usually send soldiers who ask for a discharge to the mental hospital. We will send you there."

"I have no objection," I replied. "My desire is to preach the good news to everyone, especially to those who have never heard the gospel. If there is no one preaching in the mental hospital, then I'm willing to go there. I will pray for them, and many of them will be healed and believe in Jesus."

"That will just cause more headaches," he snapped. He habitually scorned my faith in front of his military colleagues, and he delighted in relentlessly ridiculing me when he found me alone. Later, however, when he saw the genuineness of my conviction to resign, he gave me an American coat and sent a military truck to take my belongings to Katra.

The commanding officer spoke up. "Vargis, you say that Jesus is the only God. What evidence do you have to prove it? How can you say that other incarnations are not God?"

The Lord filled my mouth, and I boldly declared, "Sir, there are more than 1,200 soldiers and 1,800 civilians working under you. They all believe and worship different deities. Not one of these soldiers or civilians can say he has received forgiveness for his sins through his gods. There is no evidence to support it. But you know me. I used to smoke heavily, and I was a drunkard and a thief. Then one day I believed in Jesus, and He saved me from all my sins. Only the true God can do that. After I was saved, I shared the way of salvation with others, and many of them also became believers. Some of them are in this unit."

"Who are they?" he inquired.

I gave him the names of several who had been saved.

"There are also others who have found peace in the Hindu gods," he said. "Just look at Swami Vivekananda!"

"It is difficult to talk about a person who lived before we were born," I countered. "Besides, that's just one person. I can tell you about many people who are living right now who have been saved recently."

They dismissed me and sent my request to the brigadier, who read it and underlined the word "evangelization." In the margin he wrote, "What is this? A disease? Where is the medical certificate?"

The following day I was called into his office, where I saw a man I had shared the gospel with in the military hospital. He told the brigadier what the word *evangelization* meant, and the brigadier smiled and signed the paper.

The discharge process was a long ordeal that required me to go to several different offices in different places. Once the necessary papers were signed at each stop, I had the rest of the day off and would go off into the nearby hills to fast and pray. I'd sit under the cool shade of a large rock and pray the afternoon away.

During those long hours of prayer, I felt a nearness to God that was unlike anything I had ever experienced. In the evenings, I would return to where I was staying or meet up with my friend George to pray.

OBEDIENCE IS GREATER THAN SACRIFICE

One night during the discharge process, I was sleeping soundly when I felt someone shaking me awake. I opened my eyes, but no one was there. I went back to sleep, but was awakened again. Finally I said, "Is it You, Lord?"

The Lord said, "Wake up and pray."

Tired and sleepy, I argued that I had been praying all day, and crawled back under the covers and fell asleep. The Lord woke me up a third time, so I sat up on the bed. I had no idea what to pray for, so I began to praise Him. As I worshipped, a vision unfolded like a movie.

I was standing in Cannaught Place, Delhi's most prominent shopping center. It was a chilly night and I was in my suit. One of my alcoholic friends was with me, and we'd walked into a stationary store where I knew the owner. "I need a good pen," I said after I greeted him. He turned to the salesman and said, "Show him a few of our good pens."

As he spread them out before me, I picked up one with a gold cap and slipped it into my pocket. After looking at all the pens, I said, "I don't like any of these," and left the shop.

As the vision ended, the Lord asked, "Do you remember that, Vargis?"

"Yes, Lord, I do remember it," I replied with regret. "But I had been drinking at the time."

"I know," the Lord responded, "but on your way to get your papers signed, I want you to go through Delhi, return to that shop, confess your sin to the owner, and pay for the pen."

I didn't know how I could do it. The owner knew me very well, and if I were to confess to stealing the pen, it would bring me great dishonor. So pleading with the Lord to understand, I said, "That happened before I was saved! You assured me that my sins were forgiven and erased from Your memory. Why are You bringing it up again?"

The Lord responded immediately, saying, "Because you must make restitution in order for Me to bless you, to bless your ministry, and to make your life a blessing. For these things to happen you need a guilt-free heart."

I sat for a long time wondering how I could do the things God was asking me to do. On the one hand, I had a deep desire to confess my sin and make it right. On the other, the thought of being looked upon as dishonorable made me weep.

Wishing to make a bargain with the Lord, I said, "This is very difficult for me. Instead, I will give fifty rupees to an orphanage."

Not willing to bargain, the Lord asked, "If you give fifty rupees to an orphanage, will the owner get his money for the pen?"

Still looking for a way out, I said, "Okay, Lord, I will give five hundred rupees to build a new church building."

But the Lord would not be persuaded. In desperation I came up with another idea. "Lord, that pen didn't even cost twenty-five rupees. I'll send it by money order."

Again the Lord was adamant. "That's not enough. You need to go personally to the store owner, confess your sin, and pay for the pen."

I knew it was fruitless to continue arguing, so I began to praise Him, though my praises seemed to go no higher than the mosquito net above my bed. I slept, but when I awoke the next morning, the joy of my salvation seemed to have drifted off with the morning breeze. I sensed a shift in my relationship with God, but I consoled myself by thinking things would improve during the day as I fasted and prayed.

I went to the hillside to pray as usual, but the shade of the rock was little comfort. I began to praise God, but I felt uneasy in my spirit. My prayers seemed to fall to the ground because my relationship with the Lord had been altered.

Anguish overwhelmed me as I tried to imagine my life without the sweet fellowship with God that I was learning to enjoy. Finally I couldn't stand it any longer. Bursting into tears, I cried, "Lord, please give back to me the joy of my salvation. I will obey whatever You command me to do. I will go to the shop, confess my sin, and make restitution."

As I spoke those words of obedience, the heavens seemed to open and shower blessings on me like drops of perfume. I was baptized in celestial joy, and as tears streamed down my face, I began to sing.

I have no idea how long I sang. I experienced a vision in which I was walking with Jesus, and the love of God was filling my heart to overflowing. When I eventually opened my eyes, I saw a man in rags staring at me. I smiled at him.

He spoke in Telugu, a language I didn't speak. I asked him to speak in Hindi, but he couldn't understand me. With signs and gestures, he asked if I was hungry. I replied in Hindi and used gestures to indicate that I was a soldier in the army and had plenty of food.

"Do you not have enough money?" he asked.

"I get paid next week," I said. "I will get a lot of money."

"Then why do you laugh and cry at the same time?"

With great difficulty, I communicated the message that I was a sinner who used to smoke and drink heavily. "Then I heard about Jesus, who is God, and I prayed to Him and received Him into my heart. He changed my life, gave me peace unlike anything I have ever known, and filled me with great joy. That's what you just saw."

The man knelt down and began to pray. He reached into his pocket and pulled out tobacco and matches and flung them away. He raised his arms toward heaven, and right there, he received Jesus as his Lord and Savior.

The Lord taught me a great lesson in obedience that day. He will bless His children abundantly if only we will obey without any doubt. I obeyed the Lord, and he saved a man named Kesav with whom I could hardly communicate.

RELEASED TO BE A BOND SERVANT

Later on that same day, I stood before the records officer who gave me a final certificate of discharge and the money due to me. He showed me all the documents pertaining to my military service and the discharge certificate, which stated that my character was "exemplary." When everything was completed, he handed me an official certificate of recommendation—a document that would facilitate my reemployment and make me a preferred candidate for a nonmilitary job anywhere in India.

I immediately tore up the papers. The officer exploded in fury and asked me why I had done such a foolish thing. "I don't need another job," I explained. "I am going to serve Almighty God. I didn't resign from the army in order to find another job. I was an immoral man, but Jesus saved me. Now I'm going to do His work, which doesn't require a job certificate." I gave him the last salute of my military career, and then I turned and walked out of his office.

In truth, I was afraid I would be tempted to find another job if my wife and child were starving. Until that day, everything I needed had been provided—good food, soft bedding, a monthly salary, free medical treatment, free train tickets, and much more. I knew that I had to burn any bridge that would tempt me to turn my back on the Lord's work.

It took twenty-eight days, but I was finally released from the army, despite the fact that the reason listed for my dismissal was not within the military rules.

Sergeant Vargis, a full-time soldier of the Indian Army, became Brother Vargis, a full-time soldier of Jesus Christ.

GIVING ALL FOR HIS SAKE

Now I had a new dilemma. What should I do with all the money I had received from the army? One friend suggested I put it in an account to draw interest. Another suggested that I use half the money to buy some land and save the rest for my children's education. Still another suggested that I buy some land for my heirs to claim later.

While any of these ideas might have seemed practical, Lilly and I felt that the Lord was leading us in a different direction. We reasoned that if we were now trusting God for our daily needs, we could also trust Him with the future education of our children.

We ultimately decided to distribute the money among several Christian organizations. I left no safety net for my family, reasoning that a life of faith begins immediately, not tomorrow.

I resolved then and there to walk to my "promised land" with my pockets empty but my heart full of faith in God. The adventure had begun.

Faithful Is He Who Calls You

Are you passionate about obeying the call of God on your life? Did you know that as you step out in obedience to that call, He promises to steer you in the right direction, open doors for you, and fill you with kingdom purpose? It's true! Consider the following scriptures:

- *Your ears shall hear a word behind you, saying, "This is the way, walk in it," whenever you turn to the right hand or whenever you turn to the left* (Isaiah 30:21 NKJV).

God will be faithful to tell you which path to take. As this verse indicates, He will speak plainly, should you begin to veer off course. You can rest in the fact that He knows where He's leading you and will guide you with clarity and accuracy.

- *He opens doors, and no one can shut them; he shuts doors, and no one can open them* (Revelation 3:7 NLT).

God will be faithful to open the specific doors you need to walk through to accomplish His will. If you will confess this scripture over your life, He'll not only open the right doors, He'll also close any others that could lead you down the wrong path.

- Jesus warned in Luke 9:62, *"No one, having put his hand to the plow, and looking back, is fit for the kingdom of God"* (NKJV). The inverse of this scripture is just as true: "Anyone who puts his hand to the plow and does *not* look back, *is* fit for the kingdom of God."

God will be faithful to fill your life with purpose. The word *fit* means to be "appointed, ordained, purposed, or conceived."* So as you put your hand to the plow, God will sow seeds of kingdom purpose into your life. The longer you persevere in your walk with Him, the more you will understand His plan and see it come to fruition.

Be encouraged today! You have appointments and assignments ahead that will yield great fulfillment and reward. Press on. Declare the Word over your situation. Then step out in obedience to His call each day. As you do, He promises to be the Voice behind you that guides, the Door that opens the way, and the Purpose compelling you onward—for *faithful is He who calls you, and He also will bring it to* pass (1 Thessalonians 5:24).

> *Father God, I yearn to fulfill Your call on my life. Attune my ears, that I might hear Your voice clearly. Guide my steps, that I might press forward in full confidence, knowing You will surely bring to pass that which You've promised. I trust You to open the doors for me that need to be open, no matter how tightly they've been shut—and to keep closed the doors You would not have me walk through. I set my hand to the plow. Strengthen and enable me as I persevere. My heart is full of faith, and I put my trust in Your Word, praying these things in the name of Your Son, Jesus. Amen.*

---

* *Biblesoft's New Exhaustive Strong's Numbers and Concordance with Expanded Greek-Hebrew Dictionary.* Copyright © 1994, 2003 Biblesoft, Inc. and International Bible Translators, Inc.

Chapter 6

GOD'S TRAINING GROUND

Teach me Thy way, O Lord, and lead me in a level path.
—Psalm 27:11

So it was that in September 1972, I became a full-time missionary. There was no question that God had called me to Katra, though I was terrified to go. Not only was it a place of pilgrimage for thousands of devout Hindus, but it was also a place without Christians. I didn't know of a single Christian in the entire population. I begged God to send a more experienced evangelist to that city and to send me somewhere else, but He wasn't persuaded by my pleas. His Spirit compelled me to go to Katra—so I packed up all my doubts and fears, and went.

I had arranged for some other Christian workers to go with me, but because of delays in their plans, I had to keep postponing our departure. By the end of October, my spirit was restless, and I couldn't postpone going any longer. Making it a matter of prayer, I said, "Lord, everyone who agreed to go with me is busy. Will You go with me?" I heard an inner voice say, "I go to Galilee before you. There you will see Me."

Knowing that I would not be alone, I told Lilly, "I'm going to Katra today even if no one else comes with me. Jesus has promised to go before me." Then I packed a few essentials and a bundle of tracts for the journey.

GOD CONFIRMS HIS CALL

As I resigned myself to going alone, a lovely, devout Christian woman named Christy Thomas (my pastor's wife) came to me and said, "Brother Vargis, when I prayed about your upcoming trip, the Lord prompted me to read John 16:32. It says, *'Yet I am not alone, because the Father is with Me.'* I believe it is God's message for you."

She picked up her devotional, *Streams in the Desert*, and read this passage to me:

> "It isn't always easy to put our convictions into practice. Along with the necessary separation and sacrifices you are making will come losses and loneliness. But those who, like eagles, soar to heights where there are no clouds and bask in the sunshine will find satisfaction even in the midst of loneliness. The eagle is unique. They fly alone and not in flocks, but they inhabit the high places, far above the clouds. Likewise, those who live for God forsake the company of others and experience the presence of God.
>
> "God is seeking eagle-like men. Those who enjoy the good things of God are people who walk alone with God. Abraham was alone in Horeb. Lot was alone in Sodom. Moses, who had all the wisdom of Egypt, had to spend forty lonely years with God. The Apostle Paul, who was a Greek scholar, had to be in the desert to learn from God. In this loneliness God teaches us to trust Him.
>
> "We need the help and encouragement of others, and there is a place for that in the Christian's life. But at times these may become

hindrances to our faith. God knows how to change our situation to give us loneliness. When we surrender our lives to Him, He will lead us through various experiences. After that we will know that we do not need the help of those who loved us. Then we will understand that He has given us something and that He has taught us to soar to the heights of the sky.

"We should be willing to be lonely. Jacob had to be alone so that God could whisper in his ears. Daniel had to be alone to have the heavenly vision. The Apostle John had to be alone on the Isle of Patmos to see the writings of heaven. Are we ready for loneliness?"*

When she finished reading, I knew that God's direction was clear. I had to go alone.

HE KNOWS OUR NEEDS BEFORE WE ASK

The next morning, after eating a light breakfast, I boarded a bus and was in Katra by ten thirty. I walked up and down the main roads, looking for a place to stay. There were vacant houses everywhere, but as soon as the owners of these houses found out I was a Christian, they refused to rent to me. In those days, Christians were considered to be on the same level as scavengers (and still are today in Kashmir). It was getting late, and I'd been lugging the box of tracts and booklets all day. I'd been looking for a room for five agonizing hours, and I was exhausted. Finally, in desperation, I stood in an intersection and cried out in prayer, "Lord, You wouldn't be wandering around these streets. If You have truly come before me, then I believe that You have arranged for me to find a place to stay. Please show me that house."

---

* *Streams in the Desert, Volume 1,* © 1925, 1953, 1965 by Cowman Publications Inc. Published in India by permission of Zondervan Publishing House, Grand Rapids, p.384, December 20 devotion.

Just then a young man called to me from across the street, "Do you need a room?"

I couldn't believe my ears! "What?" I stammered.

He looked at me intently, and realizing that I was South Indian, he said in English, "Do you want a room?"

I was overcome with relief and joy. I'd been wandering around town for hours, and now this stranger was asking me if I wanted a room! "Yes, I want a room!" I shouted.

He assumed that I was one of the pilgrims and asked how many days I would be staying. I told him the truth, "I am a preacher of the Lord Jesus Christ, and I have come to stay. I need a permanent room."

He picked up my bag and led me to a nearby tea shop where he bought me a glass of milk. "You are my older brother, and I am your younger brother," he said. "Stay here, and I will go and make arrangements for your room."

He returned a few minutes later and said, "Come with me. I've found two rooms for you, and you need to choose the one you would like."

I was stunned. I'd reached the end of my strength, but when I called upon the Lord and put the situation into His hands, He provided a room. And not just one . . . but two! This was a welcome confirmation that He was with me. Even now, all these many years later, when I pass that place, I shed tears of joy and praise God for what He did for me that day. It might seem like a small thing, but it was the confirmation I needed to rest in the assurance that He was with me.

FAITH THAT PLEASES GOD

Happy with the Lord's provision after a long and exhausting day, I quickly settled into my room and decided to go to the Katra bus terminal to pass out tracts. The station was teeming with visiting pilgrims, and many who were curious took the tracts and bought the small booklets to read.

Because I was new in the Lord, I felt ill-equipped to preach. I also knew there was no way I could argue convincingly with a Hindu scholar. But in a city where nearly two thousand pilgrims a day come and go, I thought I could hand out tracts and sell booklets without people asking too many questions. My hope was to reach several parts of the country as these people read the tracts and booklets and passed them on to others.

There isn't much to read in India today, and there was even less in those days; so the tracts and booklets I distributed had more than just monetary value. Very few of them ended up in the trash.

That day a beggar approached me and asked for a tract. Then he asked me to explain what it meant, so I shared my testimony with him.

"I am Mani Ram," he said. "I was a sweeper in the army for many years. While I was in the military hospital, a man told me about Jesus, and I have been curious ever since then. Will you come to my home and stay with me overnight?"

I looked at his wretched figure. He had chronic asthma, and his frail body was draped in rags and a shabby coat. He used a crude walking stick to help support him as he hobbled along. My reservation quickly gave way to compassion, and I followed him to his home, which was a single room with a cramped kitchen. His wife Rahel worked as a temple sweeper, and they had two children.

They served me chapattis (baked paper-thin wheat bread) with daal (a curry paste made of lentils). It was the first meal in my promised land, and I ate with relish.

Mani Ram invited other friends and relatives to his house to hear what I had to say. I sang a song in Hindi, gave my testimony, and delivered my sermon, the only one I knew. It was about Abraham and his obedience and willingness to sacrifice his firstborn son at God's command.

After I finished ministering, I asked, "Who will decide to follow Jesus today?" Two hands went up. I led Mani Ram and his wife in a prayer of repentance.

After our prayer, Mani Ram came to me and said, "Please pray for my wife. She is possessed by an evil spirit. I have taken her to many magicians, but none of them could help her."

"The Lord will heal her," I assured him. And as I laid my hands on her and prayed, the evil spirit cried out and left her. Like the apostles sent forth in Mark 3:15, I knew that I had been given *authority to cast out the demons.*

My first day's ministry was a success! Jesus, who had gone before me, had arranged a house, brought two people into His kingdom, and compelled an evil spirit to depart on that first night. It was too wonderful to believe!

The family had two beds, and they offered one to me. The next morning as I was about to leave, Mani Ram grabbed a handful of coins from the pocket of his dingy beggar's coat that hung on the wall. Placing the coins in my hand, he said, "All are for you."

I hesitated for a moment. Born in a well-to-do family, the son of a rubber plantation superintendent, I felt uncomfortable receiving money earned as alms. Then a thought struck me. My Teacher, Jesus, never hesitated to accept anything that was offered, regardless of who gave it to Him. I didn't want to deny Mani Ram his blessing, so I gratefully pocketed the coins.

I was jubilant! The first twenty-four hours of my missionary journey had been very rewarding. Two souls won for the kingdom, one soul released from Satan's bondage, and a handful of coins for God's messenger!

Take Nothing with You

I returned home the next day and prepared to move Lilly and Aby to Katra. We loaded the inside and top of the bus with our household belongings and ten bundles of gospels, tracts, and booklets for distribution.

I barely had bus fare for two, but after our Sunday worship service, the pastor had handed us forty rupees. That had certainly lightened the mental strain because I needed to pay the landlord exactly forty rupees to cover our rent. We had also received some other gifts, and I'd used some of the money to buy a 50 kg bag of high-quality American rice from the military canteen. I thought it might come in handy if food and money became scarce. The very thought of the rice supply helped me breathe a little easier.

After arriving in Katra, we unloaded our things from the bus, and I spent two rupees to buy some milk for Aby. When we were settled in the room, I poured some kerosene in the stove and turned to Lilly, "You can give the milk to Aby. And I am really hungry, so please cook some of the rice for me. By the way, we are almost out of money. It's a good thing I bought that rice, or we'd be starving right now."

Lilly stopped in her tracks, her face registering shock. "Rice?" she asked as she stared at me wide-eyed. We frantically searched the room, but the rice sack had seemingly vanished into thin air.

"The rice is still on the top of the bus. We forgot to unload it!" she wailed.

Frantic, I rushed to the bus stop, but no one could give me any information. The buses were on fixed routes that ran weekly, not daily, and that particular bus would not be back for two weeks. I was sure that the rice was lost for good. I felt like crying. There was hardly any money left. *What will we eat?* I wondered.

Devastated, I went back to my room, fell prostrate before the Lord on the cold, bare concrete floor, and wept. Immediately the Lord asked me, "Son, didn't you say you trusted in Me and wouldn't store things for the future? Why did you buy a provision of rice and betray your steps of faith?"

"Yes, Lord. But I was able to buy some quality rice from the military store," I argued. Even as I spoke, I knew that it was a weak rationalization. I also knew that I had bought the rice as a precaution…just in case. My plan had failed, and as I lay alone before God, my heart was revealed to me. I prayed for quite some time and asked the Lord to forgive me. Then

I pledged, "Like the Israelites, I will gather only enough manna for the day." Then I got up and went to buy some lentils with the last few coins in my pocket.

The next afternoon I went to the bus station, where I sold a few gospel booklets by shouting, "Find out how I got peace! Read this book and receive peace!" I was able to sell enough books to buy some more food.

On the twenty-ninth day after arriving in Katra, I took ten-month-old Aby with me to distribute gospel tracts because Lilly wasn't feeling well. As I was passing out tracts, a man came up and started playing with Aby. "Do we know you?" I asked.

He smiled. "You don't remember me? About a month ago I was the driver on the bus that brought you here. Your wife and son were sitting behind me, and this little fellow was imitating me."

I asked him if he knew anything about the bag of rice, but he assured me that he didn't have any idea what I was talking about. I shared my testimony, and he was astonished by my story. He couldn't understand how a man could give up a good-paying job in the Indian Army and his wife leave a teacher's job to come to Katra to distribute booklets.

Then I said, "If I hadn't lost that bag of rice, it would have fed me for twenty-eight days. But today is the twenty-ninth day and, even without that bag of rice, my family and I haven't gone hungry a single day. My God has taken good care of us for twenty-nine days, and He will take care of me in the future as well."

The driver broke down and told me that the rice was in the conductor's house, unopened. He said he would bring it to me the next day. Sure enough, the next day he was at the bus stop, and I got the bag of rice. I gleefully carried it home on my head, shouting, "Hallelujah to the Lord!" and crying tears of joy the whole way. The Lord had taken away the rice to teach me to depend solely on Him. It was a lesson I learned well.

FAITHFUL IN THE SMALL THINGS

Lilly and I worked very hard. Every day I went to the bus stop at six in the morning to pass out tracts to the passengers. I was often without shoes and experienced the bone-chilling discomfort of northern-India winter; but I knew the agony I felt was nothing, compared to the agony the Lord feels over even one lost soul.

Around nine o'clock each morning, I returned home for breakfast and prayer before going out again to pass out tracts from ten until noon. From noon until one o'clock, Lilly taught the children of the scavengers. These people, God's creatures all, were considered the lowest class of people in India.

The caste system, still very much a reality in Indian culture, began as a way for the invading light-skinned Aryans to avoid integration with the indigenous dark-skinned people. Castes evolved to serve the same purpose unions are supposed to serve today—to protect workers and preserve the distinct characteristics found within individual communities.

Before antibiotics and antiseptics existed, health concerns necessitated that only one group of people do the work of handling carcasses and other possible contaminants that could infect the general population. In this way, the caste system also functioned as a means to help curb the spread of disease.

Once castes became a matter of heredity, social taboos grew more and more rigid, and a vast network of sub-castes, inextricably linked to occupation, became the norm. These hundreds of groups are graded on a "scale of purity," with the Brahmin priests positioned at the top and the "untouchables," who are actually considered below the castes, resting squarely on the bottom.

Because the people in the areas where we were working considered Christians to be in the same class as scavengers, the high-caste people would not allow us into their homes. So we stood in the courtyard, singing, reading Bible verses, preaching, and praying for the sick.

In the afternoons, I handed out more tracts, and in the evenings, Lilly and I dedicated ourselves to go to five different houses and share the gospel. Since I didn't know how to preach yet, I shared my testimony, prayed for those who were sick, and left a book in each home.

I spoke Hindi with a South Indian accent, which sometimes created a problem. One particular day as I was talking to a family about the Lord, a woman speaking in her native tongue asked me what I wanted.

Hoping to converse with a male family member, I asked in Hindi, "Is there a man here?" The woman didn't answer, so when another woman joined us shortly thereafter, I pointed to my face and asked, "Is there a man like me with a mustache and beard?"

The women smiled at Lilly, and I realized they hadn't understood me.

"What is the matter?" the younger woman asked.

Once again I tried to make them understand. "We have good news! We pray for the sick, and they are healed from whatever afflicts them."

The women talked with each other for moment and then hurried off to the back yard.

Meanwhile, I began praying that some men would show up. But in no time at all, the women returned . . . with a female buffalo! They had obviously mistaken the word "man" for "buffalo"; so, not knowing what else to do, Lilly and I prayed for the animal, gave the family a gospel tract, and left. We learned later that the buffalo had been sick and that God had healed it after we prayed.

Over and over again, God healed people, chickens, cattle, water buffaloes—everything!

DIVINE PROTECTION

One evening, a woman began following us from house to house as we ministered. When we were through and started home, she wanted to know if we would be doing the same thing the next night. When I told her yes, she asked which house we would start with because she wanted to come and hear the message again. She followed us every evening, diligently listening to the gospel. After three months, she came to me and said, "I am from the mountains, and it's time for me to go back. But I will be going back a Christian." I asked her name and told her she needed to be baptized. She asked what that was. I quickly described the event and its significance. It was the winter season, so I told her we would baptize her on April sixth. She didn't know what a month was. All she knew about were the three seasons in India: winter, summer, and monsoon. So, on a piece of paper, I drew a calendar. Then I gave her the calendar and a pencil, told her to mark off one date every day, and to come back on the fifth of April. Indicating that she understood, she went home.

When she returned on the fourth of April, I asked her why she had come a day early. With sincerity and great excitement, she answered, "I was afraid that I might not have marked off a date, and I didn't want to take a chance and miss my baptism day."

After I baptized her, we had communion on the veranda of our house. As she stood to leave, she said, "I have a request to make of you. I have seven boys. Will you come and tell them about Jesus so they may also go to heaven?" I asked her where she lived, and she said it was a thirty-mile walk over five mountains from the bus station. I assured her that I would come, and a few days later I grabbed my backpack and jungle shoes and started the journey.

When I finally reached the woman's village, I discovered that her sons were suspicious of me. Wondering why a stranger would walk thirty miles to see their widowed mother, they thought I was up to no good and decided to kill me.

The next morning when I went to a nearby pond to brush my teeth, the woman was hiding in the bushes so that her children wouldn't see her. "Padre, Padre, you have to run away immediately because my sons are coming to kill you!"

Knowing I had no time to waste, I grabbed my backpack and took off running. I realized that even with a head start, the boys would soon overtake me because they were young and strong and knew the mountains well. When I got to the top of the second mountain, I looked back and saw that they were gaining on me.

As I turned again to run, I stumbled on the root of a tree. I'd had nothing to eat for more than a day, and in my haste to flee, I hadn't taken time to fill my canteen. So, thinking my life was as good as over, I fumbled in my backpack for something to write Lilly a farewell note on. Scribbling a few words, I told her I was willing to die for the sake of the gospel, provided God would get one soul for each drop of my blood.

Just as I finished writing the note, I heard a chicken nearby, and as I glanced up, I spotted a house. So I quickly made my way there, found the owner, and a bought some eggs from him. With no time to spare, I ate the eggs raw and gulped down as much water as I could before taking off running again.

Somehow, I managed to make it to the bus terminal without the boys catching me. Three days later, when I was back home, I told Lilly that I would never go there again.

A few days later, the woman's oldest son showed up at my door. When I asked what I could do for him, he said, "My mother has sent me for you. She wants you to come back and preach the gospel to us."

Assuming his request was part of a plot, I told him I wasn't ready to return to the village.

"Then I will stay until you change your mind. My mother said you conduct meetings every evening. Is that true?"

"Yes, it is true," I replied.

"Where will you be tonight?" he asked. "My mother told me I must come and hear the gospel you preach, because that's what she did when she was here."

I told him where I would be that night and, not surprisingly, he came. As I preached, I watched him out of the corner of my eye, and I saw that he was crying. His behavior went on like this for several days. I would preach, and tears would stream down his face. But his tears did not move me. I was certain he was putting on an act so that I would go back to his village where he and his brothers could kill me.

Finally the Lord spoke to me. "Vargis, follow that young man and go to his house."

"God, do You want me to die?" I quickly protested.

Though I asked Him repeatedly, the Lord's answer was always the same. "I want you to go," He said.

So, knowing I must obey God, I instructed the young man to go home and told him that I would return to his village in two days.

When I later explained to Lilly that I would be going back to the village after all, I told her there was a possibility I might be killed. I wanted to be upfront, so I spoke candidly, giving her specific instructions about what she was to do in case I didn't return. "Don't go back to South India. Don't ask me how you will live without anyone to support you because I don't know. Promise me that you will instill a vision for missionary work in our son. His blood must boil whenever he hears about unreached people."

What a difficult request. But, trusting the Lord, Lilly agreed.

I then kissed her with what I thought could be the last kiss I would ever give her. Next I gathered my backpack, some soft lentils, and a canteen. Then I took the bus to the stopping point and began the long walk to the village.

I finally reached the mud-and-rock house, certain that this would be my last evening on earth. Yet to my surprise, everyone was happy and rejoicing. I went to a nearby stream to bathe, and when I returned, they asked if I was hungry. In all honestly, I was famished after the long journey. But because I was afraid the food was poisoned and I wanted to preach before I died, I told them I would eat after the meeting.

Since it is very dark on the mountains at night, the people often go to bed after eating their evening meal. But if they need to stay awake—as was the case that night—they use bunches of pine wood splinters to make torches.

Hanging on the walls of the house were several axes and knives of varying sizes, implements normally used for chopping firewood and making torches. I wondered if they would be using one of those to chop off my head.

I closed my eyes and began to pray, but as soon as I did, some chickens began clucking and flapping their wings. Suddenly there was a great commotion. My eyes flew open and I abruptly stopped praying, only to see that everyone in the room was shaking and praying simultaneously in different languages.

I had heard of people praying in the spirit, but I hadn't believed it because I hadn't yet heard of the baptism of the Holy Spirit. Yet there I was, watching all the people shaking and praying under the power of the Spirit in a language I had never heard before.

"Stop! Stop! What are you doing?" I asked. "What language are you speaking?"

The mother spoke up. "Didn't my son tell you?"

"Tell me what?" I asked.

"About the day they were chasing you. They decided to stop and drink some liquor, and when they realized it was too late to chase you, they came home. I was in my room praying that the Lord would send His angels to protect you. When my sons entered my room, they came under the conviction of the Holy Spirit. One after the other, they knelt down and cried, saying, 'Mama, I'm a sinner. I misunderstood you! That man must be a man of God! Oh Mama, I am so sorry.'"

With great excitement, she continued. "All of my sons cried and repented, their wives came and repented, and their children came and repented. As they cried in repentance and sorrow, we all received power and began speaking in God's language."

What I was sure had started out as a death march ended in celebration, for that day I had the privilege of baptizing thirteen Spirit-filled believers in a nearby stream!

As soon as I returned home, I began reading the book of Acts with a new thirst in my spirit. If people who had never heard about such an experience could have it, I wanted it too. So, with my whole heart, I sought the baptism in the Holy Spirit. And it wasn't long until God satisfied my longing. Acts 10:34 tells us that *"God is not one to show partiality."* What He did for me, those mountain people, and thousands of other hungry hearts, He will do for anyone who asks and believes.

SOWING INTO FERTILE SOIL

Some time later, a man and his wife came to me and asked if I was PG Vargis. I could tell from their clothes and smell that they were from the mountains. I told them I was the man they were looking for. Then I invited them in and motioned for them to sit on the blanket. In those days we didn't have any chairs, but they were afraid to sit on the blanket and started to sit on the floor. I insisted that they sit on the blanket, and as they moved to sit, the man said something to his wife. She pulled a large metal jar wrapped in cloth from behind her and handed it to me.

"What is it?" I asked.

"It's butter. Pure butter."

I looked into the jar and saw black goo that looked like engine oil from an old automobile. Before I could say anything, the man spoke up. "We heard about Jesus from Hannah. She has seven sons, and you baptized the whole family. Hannah told us about Jesus, and we came to believe in Him too." Then he told me about his sons, and pleaded with me, "Please come to our village and preach the gospel. I know it is a long way from the bus terminal, but if you will eat this butter, it will give you the strength to walk. I want our sons to become Christians too, but I don't know how to preach. Will you come?"

Of course I went and preached (without the aid of the "butter"), and the sons received Christ. I also preached in many other mountain villages, but there are hundreds of others who still need someone to come and tell them about Jesus.

First Fruits of Our Labors

We continued to work hard, and with tears of frustration, we pleaded with the Lord to give us the ability to speak different languages so that people could hear the gospel. Over the years, those prayers have been answered.

Lilly's class for the scavenger children grew to a regular attendance of about twenty-four. Using the gospel of Mark, she taught them the Hindi alphabet and words. She also taught them Christian songs, choruses, and Bible verses. Before long, twelve children were saved! We didn't have much food, but each day, one of the children would take a turn and eat with us.

Lilly tenderly cared for the children—bathing them, combing their hair, washing their clothes, and showing them love in every way possible. These children—not allowed to enter the homes of others—came into our home and ate with us. They couldn't believe it! They loved us and we loved them. Their parents watched us closely, and as we told them about Jesus the Savior, many of them were saved.

In April, when the weather allowed, eighteen people were baptized. The next month eighteen more were baptized...and eighteen more the month after that. In a period of four months, seventy-six people were baptized; after six months, a hundred. An Acts 2 revival was beginning to break out. Those little sheep began talking about Jesus and seeing signs and wonders!

Missionaries from other organizations had never baptized more than a dozen people—even after a lifetime of work. No one thought the results we were having were possible. Some people actually came to see if the reports were true. One American missionary who received my news-letter was convinced I was lying. She came to confront me and tell me that I should be truthful, but when she arrived at our meeting and saw a hundred people praying and praising God, she knew the conversions were genuine. The glowing, joy-filled faces testified to the fact. So the missionary stood up in our meeting and said, "I came because I was convinced that Vargis was lying, but now I know that everything he said is the truth." She apologized for thinking ill of me.

CHILDLIKE FAITH

The first people in the water at the initial baptism in April were Mani Ram and his wife, Rahel. Even though Rahel was a temple sweeper, she began to witness and distribute tracts while she worked. The temple authorities warned her that she would lose her job if she didn't stop talking about Jesus. Unable to stop recounting what God had done for her, she soon found herself jobless but full of joy. She was delighted and grew more faithful to her Savior, despite her suffering.

Mani Ram and Rahel decided to go to her childhood home with their grandchild to tell her family about Jesus. Their hike across the mountains under the hot sun was torturous, and it wasn't long before they became weak with hunger. With the baby cuddled to Rahel's side, they approached a house and asked for two chapattis but were turned away.

Finally Rahel said, "Pastor Vargis always tells us that if we believe for anything, our Jesus will provide it for us. Let's pray that God will give us chapattis."

Miserable with hunger, Mani Ram didn't have the faith to ask God for food, so he asked his wife to pray. As he stood by with his eyes closed, Rahel prayed, "Lord, our pastor taught us that when Elijah prayed, you gave him bread and meat every morning and evening. We are hungry, and the child is starving. We need two chapattis. Amen."

They opened their eyes and saw nothing but the barrenness of the mountains. "Let's go. God will take care of us," Rahel declared. Walking a few steps further, they were shocked when they spotted two chapattis on top of a rock! Bewildered, Mani Ram suspected that they belonged to some local shepherds. Scrambling onto a large boulder, he cried out, "Is anybody there?" Silence. Still amazed, he looked at the chapattis. They were freshly made, hot and buttered. Crying praises to the Lord, they devoured the food and continued on.

As the afternoon sun was roasting their skin, Mani Ram looked at his wife and said, "Jesus is truly our God. He saved us from our sins, and when we were hungry He provided us with food. Now let's pray for an umbrella to protect us from this unbearable heat."

Immediately Rahel prayed, "Lord, we thank You for Your provision. The heat is intolerable. We need an umbrella. Amen."

An umbrella didn't appear but, up above, a heavenly provision unfolded. An umbrella-like cloud overshadowed them. As they walked, the miracle cloud moved with them, keeping them cool under the comforting wings of God until they reached their destination. The Lord accomplished the impossible because their hearts brimmed with child-like faith!

There were times when people accused me of preaching the gospel without a call from God, but the Lord answered by giving us some of the finest believers I have ever known.

The first five years in Katra were times of hardship and utter poverty. But because the power of God was so strong that people were being saved, healed, and released from demonic possession every day, we scarcely noticed the suffering.

BAPTISM IN THE SPIRIT

Although I had felt the power of the Holy Spirit when I prayed, I had not yet received the privilege of praying in the spirit. My wife and several others had been baptized in the Holy Spirit and had received their prayer language, and I wanted this in my life as well.

In 1973, I attended a convention in central India and felt an assurance that I would receive the baptism during the sessions. Nothing happened between Monday and Saturday. On Sunday a pastor invited those who wanted the baptism to come forward for prayer. I was the first one to jump out of my seat. When he laid hands on me, I felt the power of God, but no prayer language came forth. As I began to pray silently, Luke 24:52–53 sprang to mind: *They...were continually in the temple, praising God.* Then I thought of Acts 2. The apostles didn't pray, cry, beg, or make any commitments to God—they simply praised Him. I quickly began to praise Him, acknowledging all His grace and blessings, and within moments, spontaneous words of a different language poured forth without any emotional prodding on my part. The Lord had fulfilled His promise. What I had witnessed in a dark mountain village and studied in the scriptures had become a reality for me as well.

Push Past the Fear—He's Gone On before You

Have you ever felt compelled to do something God has called you to do—but on the inside, you struggle because you feel completely inadequate to accomplish the task? That's exactly what I was experiencing when I said, "So I packed up my doubts and fears, and went."

It might seem like a contradiction that a person of faith would have doubt and fear. But even Paul, the great apostle of faith, wrestled with these two human frailties. Consider his confession in 1 Corinthians 2:3–5: *I was with you in weakness, in fear, and in much trembling. And my speech and my preaching were not with persuasive words of human wisdom, but in demonstration of the Spirit and of power, that your faith should not be in the wisdom of men but in the power of God* (NKJV).

You may ask then, what is the secret to stepping out in faith when the giants of fear and doubt loom larger than life? Perhaps the answer is twofold:

- Recognize that you haven't called yourself—God is the One who has called you, and He is the One who will empower you with the grace you need to accomplish the task.
- Realize that He's gone on before you. He's already there on the scene, waiting to meet you once you arrive.

In other words, if He has called you, He'll be right there in the situation with you, strengthening you as He works through you to accomplish His will.

Think about the instructions the angel of the Lord gave the women at Jesus' empty tomb: *"And go quickly and tell His disciples that He is risen from the dead, and indeed He is going before you into Galilee; there you will see Him. . . ." So they went out quickly from the tomb with fear and great joy, and ran to bring His disciples word* (Matthew 28:7–8 NKJV). Did you catch that? Great fear often accompanies great joy! And not only that, but He's gone on ahead of you, and you'll see Him when you get there.

So the next time you feel inadequate because of fear and doubt, remember the examples of all those who "did it afraid." If they pushed past the fear, you can too. And don't forget who it is that you're pushing toward—*He* is there, just waiting for you to show up!

> *Father, thank You that I am not inadequate just because I deal with fear. Thank You for the examples of great men and women of God who struggled with fear and doubt, but came out victorious. Renew my confidence, I pray, and help me to push past my weaknesses and step out in obedience to Your call, knowing that You will strengthen and empower me. You have called me, so I trust that You have gone ahead of me! I praise You and thank You, and pray these things in Jesus' name. Amen.*

Chapter 7

Coming Full Circle

"And brother will deliver up brother to death, and a father his child...and you will be hated by all on account of My name."
—Matthew 10:21–22

A s these amazing things were taking place in my life, there was growing opposition from my family. When I returned to Kerala to visit, they were all in religious bondage. Although there was no question that God had done a transforming miracle in my life, my family seemed content with the ceremonies and traditions of the Jacobite Church. Every one of them knew that my testimony was true, but they refused to accept what God had done for me, and thus continually asked me to join them in their prayers and worship. I didn't want to offend anyone, but I explained that I could not take part in any nonbiblical worship and that I would obey God rather than man.

At one point, in keeping with the custom in Kerala, my uncle tied a black thread around Aby's waist. It is a tradition the South Indian Hindus practice in an effort to ward off evil spirits. When I voiced my objection, he justified his actions by saying, "Even the Brethren and Pentecostals do it!"

I was not persuaded. "I refuse to participate in heathen practices, regardless of whether or not anyone else does such things," I declared, yanking off the thread and throwing it away.

During this time, my father decided to divide his property among his other three sons, excluding me because of my radical departure from the Jacobite Church. However, there were two small plots of land that had been bought with money I had sent home while I was in the army, and he told me I could have that land as an inheritance.

When my father told me his plans, I said, "It's all right with me if you divide even that land among my brothers. I have decided to live entirely by faith. My trust is in the Lord alone. Lilly understands this and agrees with me, but if you decide to give me the land I paid for with my military earnings, I will build a prayer hall!" Since there was no Protestant church in or near our village for many miles, I decided right there to donate the land to the Assemblies of God church so that my village could hear the gospel. Then I asked my father's permission to give them the land.

My father was amazed that I refused to argue over the property. As he paced up and down the veranda thinking about it, he appeared to be a bit agitated. Finally he spoke his mind. "When you gave away the money you earned from the army, you gave it as you saw fit. You didn't ask my permission then. So why are you asking it now?" He paused and after a moment pressed on with what was really weighing on his mind.

"Son, if something were to happen to you, if some evil should befall you, who would provide for Lilly and your family? If you died tomorrow, who would look after them? Where would they go?"

I smiled and said, "The God of Abraham will take care of them."

My confident statement belied my fear. I was deeply disturbed by my father's words and couldn't shake them from my mind. All I could think about was what would happen to my wife and child if something happened to me.

TURNING IT OVER

After supper and prayer, we spread our blanket and got ready for bed. Lilly and Aby drifted off to sleep quickly, but I tossed and turned as my thoughts churned. My father's words reverberated in my head, and finally I jiggled Lilly awake.

"I'm not giving the land to my brothers," I announced. "I'll apologize to them, and hopefully it won't be a problem."

Half asleep and trying to understand my agitation, her only response was, "Why?"

"Lilly, if something happens to me, where will you go? If you have the land, at least you could build a place to live and farm the wetlands to make a living." It was making more and more sense to me by the minute.

Fully awake now, my wife looked at me and laughed. "For the last three years, God has looked after us and met all our needs even when you weren't with us. You didn't buy any clothes for me, but God provided. There were so many times when we didn't have any money, but God always took care of us and met our needs. He's not going to stop taking care of us if something should happen to you. Of that I'm sure. Give the land for a prayer hall tomorrow, but for now, go to sleep."

Encouraged by my wife's faith, I told her what she needed to do if anything happened to me. Knowing the Indian customs, I instructed Lilly, "Your dowry has been paid, so you should not go back to your father's house. Neither should you go to my family since they did not give us any family inheritance." Then, speaking from my missionary heart, I said, "Don't return to South India. Go north and do whatever evangelism you can. Bring up Aby as a missionary for North India." She agreed, we prayed together, and finally at peace, I slept.

ONE BY ONE

Months later, Josh, my youngest brother, was planning to come visit us. Before he left home, my father looked at him warily and asked, "Son, if you go and visit, are you going to follow in your brother's footsteps?"

Josh held my father's hands and said, "I was born a Jacobite, and I will return a Jacobite." As it turned out, God had other plans. Josh was saved, filled with the Holy Spirit, and baptized the next week. He eventually went to Bible school and committed himself to the call of full-time ministry.

It wasn't long before my younger sister, a Roman Catholic, was converted while reading Psalm 40. In one of my visits with her, I had given her my Bible, and reading it had brought her to the light. She was baptized and became a living witness for the Lord.

In December 1975, when I went to Kerala on vacation, my younger brother Samjee was saved and baptized. In 1983, the Lord led him to resign his job and enter full-time ministry as a missionary.

Meanwhile, my father was concerned about my life of faith . . . but also amazed by it. He knew I had given the land to the Assemblies of God church. He and my mother thought we were well taken care of when they visited us in Katra. They knew we had neither a steady income nor a savings account and that we led a life that bordered on deprivation, yet they saw how all of our needs were continually met through prayer. Slowly, my parents began to believe in the God of Abraham, Isaac, and Jacob.

One morning while we were gathered for our usual prayers, my father burst into tears and cried out, "Lord, how long have You been knocking at the door of my heart, but I didn't open it? You were waiting outside in the chilly weather, Your head covered with dew. Lord, please don't pass me by! I open my heart to You right now."

On a cold March day in 1976, my father asked me to baptize him, and my mother quickly followed suit. God had proven himself faithful as I stood on the promise in Acts 16:31: *"Believe in the Lord Jesus, and you shall be saved, you and your household."*

The lone holdout was my brother Blesson. But when he was diagnosed with cancer, he also submitted his life to the Lord as I presented the gospel. A few months later, he traveled to Kashmir so that I could baptize him.

After my father was saved, he wanted to give me some property as an inheritance, but I refused. As far as I was concerned, the salvation of my parents was of far greater value than any material gain they could leave me.

Just before his death, my father changed his will and left me some property. I promptly sold it and invested the proceeds into the work of the kingdom. My resolve was confirmed, and I wrote in my Bible, "I will not amass earthly wealth. My children will be my wealth." When I go to my heavenly home, I want to be able to say, "I have no wealth but Jesus."

I have learned to live a simple life. Once my basic needs are met, all the rest goes for the Lord's work. My sincere desire is to heed the words of Jesus in Luke 18:22: *"Sell all that you possess, and distribute it to the poor, and you shall have treasure in heaven."* Again He instructs us in Matthew 6:19–20: *"Do not lay up for yourselves treasures upon earth, where moth and rust destroy, and where thieves break in and steal. But lay up for yourselves treasures in heaven, where neither moth nor rust destroys, and where thieves do not break in or steal."*

My father died on January 14, 1984, and the last word he spoke—not once but three times—was, "Hallelujah!"

My mother came to visit us in 1986, and she talked incessantly about the difference in our lives over the last ten years. She marveled, "Before, you could afford only a small cup of tea for breakfast, but today you have as much as you need."

My mother had the privilege of seeing God's blessings on our family. Three of her four sons were serving the Lord in full-time ministry, but better things were yet to come.

Trust Him to Care Completely

First Peter 5:7 teaches us that we should cast all our cares *upon Him, because He cares for* us. In looking back on those early years of learning to trust God with every need, I see how He proved this verse true in our lives. As Lilly and I released our anxieties to Him, throwing them over onto His shoulders and refusing to worry, God always came through for us.

When the Word says that He "cares for" us, it doesn't mean God feels sorry for us. It means He takes full responsibility for us. Hebrews 7:25 confirms this principle, promising that *He is also able to save to the uttermost those who come to God through Him.* The word *save* (*sozo* in Greek) means to "make whole."* So, through Jesus, God has the ability not only to give us eternal security, but also to preserve, protect, heal, deliver, bless, and restore us—totally and completely. In essence, He longs to take care of us, or "save" us, in every area.

I was compelled to trust God fully because I valued His Word above anything else. I believed when He said He would take care of all my needs, He meant it. That included the needs of my wife and children, our present and future finances, and the salvation of our entire household.

How about you? Do you trust God's Word implicitly? Do you believe He is interested in every area of your life and longs to bring about His best for you? Check your heart to evaluate your trust level:

- Are you persuaded that God will take care of you and your family, both now and in the future, as you cast every care upon Him?

---

* *Biblesoft's New Exhaustive Strong's Numbers and Concordance with Expanded Greek-Hebrew Dictionary.* Copyright © 1994, 2003 Biblesoft, Inc. and International Bible Translators, Inc.

- Are you convinced that as you store up treasures in heaven, God will meet all your earthly needs?
- Would you continue to put your trust in His Word if your closest family members or friends questioned your faith?
- Are you constrained to share the gospel with others even after your message has been rejected by some?

If your answer to any of these questions isn't a resounding yes, why not cast every care over on Him today? You can take God at His Word. If He says it, He means it! Stand on His Word today and trust Him to take care of you...*completely.*

> *Father God, as I step out in obedience to Your Word, I cast every anxiety and concern in my life over on You. Thank You that I can stand on Your promises and trust You to take complete responsibility for meeting my every need. I bless You and praise You, and I pray in Jesus' mighty name. Amen.*

Chapter 8

THE BIRTH OF INDIAN
EVANGELICAL TEAM

*Now faith is the assurance of things hoped for;
the conviction of things not seen.*
—Hebrew 11:1

THIS CHAPTER COULD ALSO APPROPRIATELY BE TITLED "THE Faithfulness of God," for we are nothing more than a marvelous example of God's enduring faithfulness.

In November 1972, when Lilly and I began the work in Katra, we christened our operation the Katra Evangelical Mission. In December, we began a regular monthly newsletter. Later on, after a few other brothers had joined us, I changed our name to Kashmir Evangelical Team because I wanted it to convey a team spirit rather that just a mission.

We worked there in Katra for five years. Those were years of testing and miracles. We had only the Lord to call upon for our every need, whether large or small. God met our need for literature through the generous donations of two mission organizations: Operation Mobilisation and Gospel Literature Services. The All India Prayer Fellowship advanced us books on credit, and I often sold these books to buy milk for Aby.

Your Father Knows What You Need

During those first years, there were many times when we were hungry. But God always came through for us, often through non-Christians, especially the wife of a Hindu priest.

Invariably, when our clothes wore out, a package with exactly the right size clothing would arrive. I remember one particular incident that happened during the severe winter of 1973. Lilly was concerned that Aby didn't have any warm clothes to wear. We had one sweater that was too small for him, so we put it on him backwards to try to keep his chest warm. Lilly also needed a pair of shoes.

It was at that time that I received a telegram asking me to pick up some used clothing. I didn't know the man who had sent the telegram, and I didn't have the money to travel to the place where the package was waiting; so I couldn't go get the package or have it sent to us.

It took a week, but I finally sold enough literature to buy a pair of shoes for Lilly. Unfortunately, they were too small, and there was no money to replace them.

Meanwhile, God was at work! Through a series of circumstances that only He could have orchestrated, the package was delivered to us. When we opened it, the first thing we pulled out was an expensive coat for Aby. Underneath it was another coat for him. Under the coats was a pair of shoes that fit Lilly perfectly. After that she joked, "My husband measured my feet and couldn't buy the right size shoes, but God knew the exact size I needed and sent a custom-fit pair through a stranger!"

SUCH AS I HAVE GIVE I THEE

About this time, the first evangelist from our hometown of Kashmir joined us—even though we had told him we were very poor. Indeed, we were so poor at that particular time that we couldn't even afford tea, and some days we resorted to sipping boiled water with salt or cumin for flavor. At one point, we ran out of food altogether.

Then one day, after we had prayed all morning, a friend of mine knocked on our door and explained that he had resigned his military position and was determined to join us in serving the Lord.

I was very frank with him about our financial situation; I told him he would be better off joining another mission organization that could help him out financially. But he could not be persuaded. Seeing his resolve, I said, "I have no money or provision to give you, but if the Lord gives me one chappati, I will give you half." Sharing all that we had with one another became the model for IET that continues to this day.

God gradually added workers to our team and, in the same cheerful way that the early Church divided their resources among themselves, we continued to share the provisions we received—whether food, clothing, or money. As the number of workers increased, God put a solid team in place. We gathered once a month for two or three days of prayer and fellowship. God continually answered my prayers for faithful, qualified leaders.

Around that time, I came across a magazine called *New Life*. I wrote to the publisher, explaining that I was a missionary in India and that, even though I couldn't afford to pay for it, I would like to receive the magazine. They sent it to me faithfully, and as I read the Bible-based teaching, I began to grow spiritually. I also read and diligently studied the Bible, not as a seminary student but as a student of the Holy Spirit.

Wednesdays were my prayer and Bible study days, and those days I spoke to no one but God—not even to my wife and son. There was a house a couple of doors down from us that had an orchard in the garden.

It belonged to the police inspector general of the state, and I went to him and asked if I could sit under his trees to study.

"How do I know you won't pick the fruit?" he asked.

"I am a Christian," I answered. "I won't steal from you. I just want to sit in a pleasant place and read my Bible and study. Then I will go back home."

He agreed. So every Wednesday, I went to the orchard, spread a blanket on the ground, and studied *New Life* magazines and then my Bible . . . *New Life* magazines and then my Bible . . . other Christian magazines and then my Bible—and along with the Holy Spirit, these became my teachers.

I learned about binding the strong man, the purpose of suffering, prosperity (or as I call it, the gospel of blessing), and God's role as Father. In India, even within the Church, there is no teaching on family life. I learned that a father is the priest of his home, and as a result, he has certain responsibilities before God. All of these concepts were foreign at first, but as I read and studied, God revealed the truth to me. Later I was able to teach these principles to countless others.

DREAMS BECOME REALITY

By 1975, with more people on board, we were able to broaden our outreach efforts, and we changed our name to Indian Evangelical Team (IET). As IET began to establish churches, we discovered that because the people had been immersed for so long in a world of false ritual and evil worship practices, they needed to hear the gospel again and again, and be involved in worshipping God on a regular basis. So we began holding meetings five to seven nights a week, a practice that continues to this day.

As a result of the calling and commitment of my fellow workers, hundreds of people in every state in northern India were saved and baptized during those days. I have been asked numerous times how we were able to baptize such large numbers of believers in so many places where other missionaries had failed. The only answer I've ever come up with is to attribute the conversions to the grace of God, committed leaders who value holiness, and the faithful prayer support of many believers.

For years, we prayed and asked God to establish a church hall in Katra. Even the children in our congregation prayed sweet prayers of faith, saying, "Lord, the earth is Your footstool, so please wiggle Your toes just a little and provide a small place to build our church." We expressed this need in our newsletters from 1972 through 1976, but no one responded. Even the small amount we managed to raise through tithes was stolen.

Despite our lack of finances, we continued to look for a suitable plot of land for the church. One day I thought I had found the ideal place. So I asked Lilly to stand with me on the land and pray in faith that God would provide it for us.

"If people see us praying, they might think we are practicing witchcraft," she replied. "Let's go home and pray privately."

Her fear was not unfounded. People had been healed as a result of our prayers, and rumors were circulating that we were practicing witchcraft, or black magic. The truth, of course, was that we were merely the vehicles of faith through which God's healing power flowed to others and brought restoration.

Later that night after a prayer meeting, Lilly and I slipped back to the plot unnoticed and prayed together. I picked up a clump of dirt, and as it sifted through my fingers, I claimed the land and asked the Lord to establish a church there. Then we thanked Him in advance for the answer He would bring.

As we walked home, an idea hit me out of the blue. I ran back and quickly buried a half-rupee coin as a token advance payment made in faith.

The next day I went back to the land with one of the team members and picked up a large rock. I handed it to him and said, "This is the cornerstone for the church. Please pray and lay the foundational stone."

His eyes widened, "Did you buy this land?"

I smiled. "Yes, by faith. I have given a coin as a deposit." I told him the price of the land, which seemed exorbitant to us both, and declared, "When the Lord gives us the rest, we can register it for IET."

So he prayed and laid the stone. Although poor, the believers began to give sacrificially. Seeing our faith, many others responded and began sending money. Before long, we paid for the land in full.

Even on the day of the sale, there was a miracle. We were short by a pittance and promised to pay it after the deal went through. It was the only solution we could come up with in order to prevent the whole transaction from falling through. That night and the next morning, we prayed for provision for the little bit we still owed. As we were on our way to finalize the deal, the wife of a Hindu priest who had persecuted us came up and asked us where we were going. When I told her we were going to register the land, she pressed money into my hands and said, "This is my donation for your church. The Lord spoke to me last night in a dream and told me to give this money to you."

It was exactly the amount we needed. Praise be to the God who sees our every need and responds. We prayed and the Lord provided.

OPPOSITION

With one problem solved, another reared its ugly head. In a clash of history and ideologies, the local people wouldn't allow us to build a church on the land. They confronted us, saying, "When the English ruled India, the Muslims bought land to build mosques, but we wouldn't let them. They had to build outside of Katra. We Hindus rule this country. We didn't allow them to build, and we won't allow you to build either."

But the great God of heaven—the God who rules and reigns—worked yet another miracle. It so happened that the chairman of the Katra Municipality who oversaw the buying and selling of land and buildings was a righteous Brahmin (Hindu priest). His youngest daughter was engaged, and the wedding was just a few days off when she became extremely sick.

She didn't respond to any of the medical treatments, black magic, or prayers to their gods, and her fever continued to rise. It just so happened that the chairman had a relative named Ratan Lal who had been saved in one of our services and baptized a few days prior to that. He told the chairman that his daughter would be healed if I prayed for her. But being an orthodox Brahmin, this man would not even consider inviting me into his home.

As the date for the wedding approached, the girl was still very sick, and the family was becoming desperate. Finally the chairman called Ratan Lal and said, "Arrange a prayer meeting in my home while I am away on business."

We went to the home, spoke to the girl about Jesus, and prayed for her. She was healed instantly.

Her father was the very chairman who, along with the municipal committee, had to approve the plan for the church to be built. When I told him what we wanted to do, he assured me that the committee would never agree. "But," he added, "you can do one thing. Give me the plans and go ahead and begin construction on your hall. If anyone asks you any questions, you can tell them the building plan is with the chairman."

The end result was a beautiful church hall and parsonage. As always, God surpassed our wildest expectations.

FOLLOWING THE CLOUD

It became increasingly clear that it was time for my family and me to leave Katra and go to a place where people had not heard of Jesus. Our work in Katra had been established, and we began looking for an able "Timothy" to entrust with the growing church.

We wrote to several missionary organizations and visited with a prospective pastor, but we were unable to find a person that we felt was adequately equipped to shepherd the flock. The search went on for so long that I began to think it might not be the Lord's timing for us to leave.

Even so, I was sending evangelists to places I couldn't go, and more and more missionaries were steadily joining our team. As a result of this growth, we felt an increasing need to establish a training center so that we could adequately equip eager young missionaries. With God's blessing, we opened the first center in April 1977.

As soon as I felt certain that it was God's plan for us to leave Katra, we followed the cloud of Jehovah Jireh and moved to Pathankot, located in the state of Punjab. By this time, the church in Katra was able to support three or four workers through tithes.

Because the Lord blessed our work, we were able to send people out to start churches in many other places. Mighty miracles became common in our meetings. While most organizations were struggling to find and keep trustworthy people, God graciously gave us able and faithful leaders.

I spent as many as nine months of the year traveling to different areas of our work and conducting meetings. The team continued to grow and flourish. The reports coming in were like those found in the Acts of the Apostles, and it thrilled my heart to see all that God was accomplishing for His glory and kingdom purposes.

At one point we dared to believe that God would help us plant two thousand churches by the year 2000. I am humbled and thrilled to report that, not only was that goal met, but it was surpassed. All the glory goes to the great and mighty God of the universe, to whom it is due.

BEERSHEBA COMPLEX

In Pathankot, we set up our office, home, and training center in a rented house. When the landlord found out we were Christians, he repeatedly asked us to leave. But because of the continued reluctance of the people there to rent to Christians, we could not find another place to house our ministry. We had a dilemma on our hands, so we enlisted our prayer partners and began praying that God would give us the land we needed to build a facility of our own.

When the late Pastor C. M. Joy, a man with a great gift of prophecy, visited us, he was struck by our frugal living and the lack of tables and chairs in our Bible school. As the Holy Spirit moved in one of our meetings, Pastor Joy prophesied, "I will bless you abundantly and give you sufficient land. Before long, you will be moving to new places."

Frankly, I didn't believe it. In those days, we had so few resources that I was wearing torn clothing and buying used saris for Lilly. When the Spirit of God spoke about land and housing facilities, I must admit that I had doubt.

A pastor from Delhi also came to visit, and he prayed for me and encouraged me to have faith in God's provision. Another pastor from Kerala came, and he was amazed at the work that was going on with the help from workers of various denominations. He looked me in the eye and said, "If you have faith to carry on this work with the nearly one hundred workers God has given you, why can't you trust God for the land as well?" His words resonated in my spirit, and our church began to pray and believe for the property we needed.

As that pastor was preparing to leave, a believer came and said he had a plot of land for sale. I smiled politely and, gesturing toward the pastor, said, "It's time for me to see my guest off, but I need 40 marlas (one marla is a 15 x 15–foot plot) of land. Please come back tomorrow."

As we walked to the train station, the pastor looked at me and said, "Why are you smiling?"

I laughed and said, "I have just agreed to buy 40 marlas of land, and I don't have any money!"

A smile spread across his face. "That's faith, Brother Vargis. What's the asking price?"

"One thousand rupees per marla." (At that time, the exchange rate for one US dollar was ten rupees.)

He nodded and said, "Well, I'll give you one thousand rupees. Now all you need is thirty-nine more people like me. Continue to pray. The Lord will supply the rest." He prayed for me and encouraged me as he boarded the train to leave.

As people began to hear about our need, the money poured in from believers everywhere. Before long, we had purchased 50 marlas (100 x 112.5 feet) of land for fifty thousand rupees, even though our initial request was for less land. Praise be to the Lord!

We hired an architect and a construction engineer who were also believers. I explained that we needed a church, an office, two dormitories for the workers and the Bible school students and, if possible, a place for the printing press—all the facilities needed for a mission center.

They drew up plans for a huge three-story building, but my plans had been for single-story buildings. I decided to discuss the matter with them, but they said, "You don't have enough land for a mission center." They walked over to the adjoining land, which was also for sale, and said matter-of-factly, "Brother Vargis, you need to buy this land too. Then you will have enough room, and we can redraw the plans."

I was afraid to even consider their proposal. How could I? Where would the money come from? I was left to my thoughts as they turned and said, "Let us know when you've bought the land, and you can have the separate buildings you want."

In the natural, it appeared we had another dilemma. The little money that had come in had been used to build three walls and two storerooms. There was no money to purchase additional land.

When our team leaders met, they wanted to see the land we had purchased. So I showed it to them and then mentioned that the adjacent land was for sale, suggesting that it would be a good idea to buy it before someone else did. They agreed, but wondered how it could possibly happen—the very thing I had been wondering as well!

FAITH AS A GRAIN OF MUSTARD SEED

There was only one thing to do. Lilly and I, along with a few other believers, stood on the compound wall and, looking to the north, saw the expanse of agricultural land. Beyond that, we could see the Himalayan hills covered with snow. As we were taking in the sights, someone spoke up and said, "We will buy that whole piece of land!"

Suddenly, as if in a vision, I saw buildings coming up from the ground. I thought about Pastor Joy's prophecy, and I was reminded of another pastor who had looked for and found ideal land for a Bible school.

Our team leaders were inspired to pray, and as we prayed, I had an assurance in my heart that the Lord had heard our prayers and that we would see the answer. Turning to Lilly, I exclaimed with a wave of my arm, "We are going to buy all of this."

Lilly, with her usual logic, said, "You don't even have the money to buy yourself a vest. How are you going to buy all that land?"

"The only way I can," I replied. "By faith. God will help us."

The next day, when my brother Josh and his wife returned from their honeymoon, I said, "Come with me right now, and I will take you on a walk of faith." We jumped on our bicycles, which were our only means of transportation, and rode out to the land adjacent to the land we had just bought. In great detail, I described the vision I'd had. I ended by saying, "Josh, let's build a church on the land we have and buy the rest of it to build offices, housing for the workers, a Bible school, and other necessary buildings." I pointed to each parcel of land as I spoke. When I got to the final expanse, I waved my arm and declared, "And this can be left as open ground for evangelical meetings."

Josh was overcome with excitement and agreed without hesitation. "Let's buy it. Let's believe God for the money to buy it all!"

"It's going to cost about one hundred thousand rupees," I cautioned, "and I don't even have enough for a down payment."

"We only need to look at what God has already done and trust Him to give us the provision we need. If you could believe Him for enough to buy the first parcel of land, why can't you believe Him for enough to buy it all? Between wedding gifts and what I have been saving to get my doctorate, I have about ten thousand rupees. I will give it to you for the down payment."

We prayed together, and when we had finished, the owner came by and quoted us his price of eight hundred rupees per marla. Later, after returning home, Lilly and I went back to the parcel of land, and I told her about the vision.

"But we don't have any money," she protested. "Why don't we try to buy just half of the land?"

I repeated my brother's admonition, "If we can believe God for half the land, why can't we believe Him for all of it?" Truly, our faith was being stretched. I took a deep breath and recounted God's faithfulness. "Remember how we couldn't afford to build even one room on the land we bought in the beginning, even though the land was ideal for building the headquarters for the team? I'm sure you remember when I picked up a handful of dirt and prayed, 'Lord, if Your name will be honored by our buying this land, give it to us. If it will spoil us, please don't allow it. If You provide it, please protect us from becoming unspiritual.'"

I couldn't stop reminding my wife of all that God had done because it was helping my own faith to recount God's faithfulness. "Remember when we told the Lord that if He gave us the land, it would be His and we would not make it our own or give it to our children?"

That evening the owner of the land came to settle the deal. Knowing that Josh was loaning me the down payment, I said, "We will give you ten thousand rupees on Monday and pay the rest as it comes in."

Although I knew that Josh would allow me to pay him back as I was able, I felt uneasy in my spirit about borrowing the money. It seemed to contradict a great step of faith, so I took the matter to the Lord in prayer.

Later in the week, I was told there was a registered letter waiting for me. I signed for it, but I didn't recognize the handwriting. It was from Saudi Arabia. The letter was from a man who had received our newsletter several years earlier, but had never felt led of the Lord to respond before. He wrote, "I have recently retired and have decided to give you a portion of the tithe from my retirement benefits. Enclosed is a check for ten thousand rupees."

In His faithfulness, God did not allow us to borrow the money for the down payment—He answered our heartfelt prayers and met our need.

THE LORD IS MY PORTION

One evening as Lilly and I were praising God for the land He had given us in different cities, the Lord brought to mind an incident that occurred after I was first saved.

I had gone home for a visit. None of my family understood my conversion, and they were very upset that we had chosen to be baptized. They did not like the fact that we shared our faith everywhere we went.

On Saturday evening, my father asked me where I would be going for worship the next morning.

"I'm going to go where the born-again people of God worship," I answered.

This was not what he wanted to hear. He tried to talk me out of my decision, and finally, seeing I would not budge, he said, "If you will come with us tomorrow morning and worship as our forefathers worshipped, you can have the ancestral property." Our ancestors had escaped persecution in Syria in the third century and had come to Kerala in boats. Our roots ran deep.

To make matters worse, my mother chimed in. "If not, we will decide who will get this house and the other property," she said.

My head spinning with the threat of being disinherited, I walked out into the courtyard. I looked around at everything my father owned and considered his wealth. He had a car and a lot of property. If I received my share of it, my future would be secure. If I did not, it would be a great loss. I knew that even if I'd made the military my career, I would never have made enough money to own as much as he did. Adding to my dilemma was the fact that, in India, the ancestral home is regarded as the heart of the family—not to mention that a lot of my money had gone into helping build it.

I was in a quandary. India is a land of tremendous poverty, so the temptation to have such abundant provision and prosperity was a huge pull. If I obeyed my father and went to his worship service, I knew it would cost me the joy of my salvation and quench the Holy Spirit within me. On the other hand, if I didn't go, I would lose all the property and wealth that would have been given to me. Joy or loss—what should I do?

I looked up at the sky, wishing for a sign. I saw nothing but the vast heavens and unchanging stars. Suddenly I remembered Abraham. Abraham had looked at the stars and believed God. Trusting that He would fulfill His promises, Abraham left behind all that he had and all that he knew to follow the Lord.

In that moment, I made up my mind. I went back into the house and told them my decision. "The Lord is my portion. I will go where the Bible is taught and people worship God with clapping and singing."

With those words said, I gave up my inheritance. Today, I have never once regretted my decision.

Great Is Thy Faithfulness

As I struggled with my decision to buy the three acres of land, the Lord asked, "If your father had given you your portion of his property, how much would have come to you?"

I did a quick mental calculation. "About 150,000 rupees."

"And what's the value of the property you have recently bought?" He asked.

Another quick calculation revealed the total to be about 150,000 rupees.

The Lord said, "You have not suffered a loss because you obeyed Me. I am the God of Abraham."

With a heart filled with thanks, I said, "Lord, I want only You as my wealth. I will not own anything, and whatever You give to me I will give back to You."

We purchased the land, and I drew the plans for the training center. We began to build with great enthusiasm, and the funds flowed in regularly. However, when we were about halfway finished, the money all but dried up.

Lilly and I went to the construction site and prayed. Sensing my frustration, my wife took my hand and encouraged me, saying, "God has brought us this far, and He will finish what He has begun."

It took nearly two years to complete the facilities, but the Lord helped us the entire way. Outside the grounds, we planted all kinds of fruit trees, including mango, fig, and orange. We hung a solid gate at the entrance and wrote above it, "THIS IS WHAT GOD DID—A SOLID MONUMENT OF GOD'S RESPONSE TO MAN'S FAITH."

It was the truth. God had provided the money to build it all when we had no resource but Him. So from that point on, we followed this pattern in all we did. Praise His holy Name!

Faith That Remains Strong

Do you have a vision for your life? A dream you long to fulfill? If your answer is yes, then rejoice! But get ready—there may be a few fiery trials up ahead. First Peter 1:6–7 explains why:

So be truly glad! There is wonderful joy ahead, even though it is necessary for you to endure many trials for a while. These trials are only to test your faith, to show that it is strong and pure. It is being tested as fire tests and purifies gold—and your faith is far more precious to God than mere gold. So if your faith remains strong after being tried by fiery trials, it will bring you much praise and glory and honor on the day when Jesus Christ is revealed to the whole world (NLT).

According to this passage, God allows you to go through trials* so that your faith will remain strong until the end. When you experience a trial, it doesn't mean you don't have *enough* faith**; it's merely an opportunity to prove the strength of your *existing* faith. During the test, if there is an area of your life that needs purifying, God will deal with you about it. He loves you so much that He doesn't want anything to remain that would contaminate your faith. He knows "faith pollutants" will cause you to grow weary and faint in your mind in the heat of the battle (see Hebrews12:3).

As you have learned in this book, before we formed IET, I was dependent on natural means for my financial security. God knew that if I continued in that mindset, I wouldn't be strong enough to believe for the miraculous when IET faced great need. So He tested me early on to see if I would trust Him as Provider. The fiery trials burned out the old way of thinking and left me with a faith so solid that I no longer put my

---

* Notice the difference in a trial and a temptation. God never tempts—He allows trials but does not set temptation before us. James 1:12–15: *Blessed is the man who perseveres under **trial**, because when he has stood the **test**, he will receive the crown of life that God has promised to those who love him. **When tempted, no one should say, "God is tempting me." For God cannot be tempted** by evil, **nor does he tempt** anyone; but **each one is tempted** when, by his own evil desire, he is dragged away and enticed. Then, after desire has conceived, it gives birth to sin; and sin, when it is full-grown, gives birth to death* (NIV; emphasis mine).

** Jesus said we could move an entire mountain with faith the size of a tiny mustard seed (see Matthew 17:20).

confidence in money or material possessions supplied by man. God alone became my source. In turn, neither fear nor unbelief could corrupt God's compelling call to reach the lost of India.

Great pilgrims of the faith have always gone through periods of testing. Joseph was such a man (see Genesis 37–45). In his youth, he received several dreams he believed would one day come to pass. Though he didn't understand the full meaning of the dreams, Joseph shared them with his brothers and father—who understood the dreams even less! In fact, Joseph's brothers thought he was not only arrogant but delusional. So they did their best to get rid of their baby brother and squelch his foolish notions forever.

But God wouldn't permit Joseph to let go of those dreams. Time and time again, when he was scorned or betrayed or forgotten, God challenged Joseph to keep on believing. Psalm 105:19 depicts God's purifying fire at work in Joseph: *Until the time that his* [Joseph's] *word came to pass, the word of the LORD tested* [refined] *him.* We're not sure what Joseph was wrestling with at that point—perhaps hopelessness or victim mentality. What we are sure of is that he withstood the test. Straight from the Refiner's fire, Joseph took his place as second-in-command of all Egypt.

It's important to note several things: First, Joseph's boyhood dreams came to pass exactly as the Lord showed him they would, and they served to anchor Joseph's faith during times of severe testing. Second, God had a much greater purpose in mind for Joseph than he first envisioned. Though he did eventually rule over his family, more importantly, he preserved a people who were destined to become a mighty nation—and from that nation came the Seed who ransomed the whole earth.

If you are experiencing a trial today, rejoice! God has a greater purpose for your life than you could ever imagine. Don't be concerned if other people judge you because you're going through a trial. And don't worry when others don't validate your dream. Stand firm in your faith. Walk in wisdom, recognizing that God only allows trials because He loves you and wants you to make it to the end. Remember, all the gold in the world could never be as precious to Him as faith that when tested, remains strong.

> *Father, I rejoice in You today! Thank You that You are at work in my life, purifying me, because my faith is precious to You. I pray that my faith would remain strong to the end and result in praise and glory and honor at the appearing of Jesus Christ. These things I lift to You in His name. Amen.*

Chapter 9

LEARNING THROUGH THE YEARS

"But when He, the Spirit of truth, comes, He
will guide you into all the truth."
—John 16:13

A S THE YEARS WENT BY, GOD TAUGHT US MANY VALUABLE lessons. He was merciful to us, keeping us away from false doctrines, even as He helped us choose the right doctrines and true faith. He taught us to believe and obey the Word of God, often against the dictates of our intellect. He grounded us to stand for holiness, even at the risk of material losses.

One thing God taught me was that He would always supply the Word He wanted me to give others. When I initially arrived in Katra, I had study notes for just one message, which I preached the first day. After the church was formed, I had to preach every day and twice on Sunday. But in all of those meetings, I never ran out of sermons and never preached the same message twice.

Another lesson He taught me began the very week I was saved. As I was singing a song from a romantic film one day, someone whispered to me, "You're saved now. That song is not for you."

Upon hearing those words, I went to the kitchen where Lilly was cooking. Because she was from an evangelical home full of saved people who preached the gospel, I thought she might have an opinion about the matter. So I asked her, "Lilly, are film songs displeasing to the Lord?"

"No," she replied, giving voice to her convictions. "You can sing clean songs. Just avoid songs that include obscene words."

Unable to get the whispered message out of my mind, I prayed about it and made the decision to obey the voice. Then I went to Lilly and said, "From now on I will never sing a song from another movie." I never have.

In His faithfulness, God continued to teach His ways to both Lilly and me. Many years ago the Lord gave us a large gift. We had already decided to live a frugal life and save whatever we could for the Lord's work. We had promised Him that we would not be expensive children. Because of our resolve, we gave up many things. We had little clothing, slept on the floor, and ate basic food. We never heated the room in winter or had air conditioning in the summer.

Yet God remained close to us in our afflictions. He was our physician when we were sick, He gave us food when we were hungry, and He was our ever-present help. To this day, we live as simply as we lived back then, continually relying on Him for our every need.

THE GOD OF THE PRACTICAL

During those days, a pastor had come to conduct a Bible class for evangelists. Lilly was cooking for over fifty people at the time, and most of them didn't help much. Some wouldn't even wash their plates after supper, leaving Lilly to do it. The visiting pastor, having observed the situation, pulled me aside and said, "Brother, why don't you hire a cook rather than wearing out your wife like this?"

"We'd have to pay a cook a salary," I replied. "For that amount of money we could be supporting an evangelist."

He looked at me thoughtfully. "Brother, which is more important—supporting an evangelist or wearing down your wife's health like this? If she gets worn down from fatigue, your ministry will come to a screeching halt!"

I knew instantly that the pastor was right, and we hired a cook for the Bible school. God taught me the valuable lesson that people are more important to God than money.

He taught me that lesson again when I was in the Middle East preaching for a few days. When I got back to the hotel after the first night's meeting, I felt a sore throat coming on. The next morning I really wanted a cup of coffee to soothe my throat, but I didn't want to pay the price the hotel charged, so I thought better of it.

I decided that I would suffer rather than ordering a cup of coffee. Later, as I was praying, the Lord said, "My son, which is more valuable to me? Your throat or the money it costs to buy a cup of coffee?"

I thought about it for a while and ordered the coffee. Afterward, my throat felt much better. God taught me that a healthy body is needed to do His work, and He reminded me of the importance of taking good care of our bodies, which are temples for His Holy Spirit.

Meeting Every Need

The Lord taught me early on that He was the source not only of my provision but of my family's as well. Just as I asked and received from God, they too were to ask and receive by faith.

Once while I was preaching out of town, Aby started a new school year. After the first week, his teacher insisted that all the children wear uniforms to school. When Aby told Lilly what the teacher had said, Lilly prayed for God's guidance. Knowing that they didn't have money to buy a uniform, she said to Aby, "Your father is not here. You will need to ask your Father in heaven to provide a uniform for you."

Aby prayed a simple yet confident prayer: "Jesus, I need a uniform by Monday, or I can't go to school. My daddy is off doing Your work, so please give me the shirt and pants I need. Amen."

That afternoon the postman came to the house with a registered letter and asked, "Who is Aby Vargis?" Lilly pointed to the boy playing in the courtyard. The postman looked at him in disbelief and insisted Lilly sign the acknowledgment.

When she opened the letter, she realized that it was from a man in Singapore who had been a supporter for over four years. Realizing that this was the first time he had written to Aby, Lilly called him over and read the letter. "While we were praying for you a few days ago, the Lord put it on my heart to send you some money. You will find a check for three hundred rupees enclosed."

"Look, Aby," Lilly sang. "The Lord heard your prayers! Now we can get your uniform."

The Lord chose *the foolish things of the world* (1 Corinthians 1:27) to meet Aby's need by prompting a man to send a check to an eight-year-old boy by registered letter.

OBEDIENCE BRINGS ABUNDANT BLESSINGS

As I continued my work in Katra, I heard about a five-week training program for pastors and evangelists, which was to be held in Singapore. I knew that pastors and evangelists who received training in foreign cities received a lot of respect when they came back with their shiny new suits, cameras, projectors, and gospel paraphernalia. A couple of evangelists that I knew planned to attend the training, and since I was still a relatively unknown evangelist, I was interested in going as well.

I applied for a passport and managed to get the difficult but necessary recommendation of an IAS officer (an official of the Indian Administrative Service). When I got back home, I was praising God profusely for helping me to go abroad. I could hardly wait to get the training and return home to greater status, new suits, and the praise of men.

Suddenly God interrupted my praise and gently asked, "Vargis, why do you want to go to Singapore?"

God has always dealt with me gently, as with a child, and I suppose I always respond to His questions like a child too. That day was no exception. "Lord, I'm going to study!" I asserted.

"What do you expect to get out of studying there?" He pressed.

"Honestly, Lord, not much," I sighed.

"Then why do you want to go?"

I was candid with God and told Him, "I need things like a tape recorder, a camera, and a typewriter."

"Why should you go all the way to Singapore for those things when you can ask Me, and I will give them to you?"

Knowing that was true, I then disclosed my other reason. "If I go to a foreign country, people will respect me more."

God didn't see it that way, and He told me not to go. I cried and begged, but it didn't do any good. He would not be persuaded. Though I was disappointed, I was determined to obey Him. So I tore up the passport application, prized officer's signature and all. Immediately the peace of God washed over me.

A few weeks later, a brother from Kerala came to visit. After we had chatted for a bit, he opened his briefcase and said, "Another brother wanted to give you this tape recorder." It was a brand-new Panasonic. A few weeks later I was given another one. I needed one, but the Lord gave me two! When I obeyed the Lord, I received a double portion. Had

I disobeyed God and gone to Singapore, I might have come home with one, but there was no guarantee.

As tears of joy welled up within, the devil taunted me, saying, "You didn't get the camera and typewriter."

"God will give them to me in due time," I replied. "And in the same way, He will give me more than I ask."

Two years later a distinguished visitor came to my office. "Where is your typewriter?" he asked.

"I don't have one. A supporter sent me the money to buy one a while back, but I used it to support my evangelists," I explained.

The man gave me a typewriter, a camera, and a tape recorder on the spot. As I was jumping with excitement, he asked me to put on my suit so he could take my picture with the camera. I had to tell him that I didn't own a suit and tie . . . and hadn't since I'd left the army.

He opened his suitcase and handed me a beautiful suit, tie, and shirt. I put them on, and he snapped the picture. When I turned to change clothes, he said, "No need to change. The clothes are yours." With those simple words and the wonderful gifts, my desire to go abroad vanished.

When I obeyed God, He blessed me . . . and blessed me abundantly. I have since preached in many foreign countries, and I receive invitations all the time to many others. Praise be to God!

His Timing Is Always Perfect

In 1985, after a conference in Switzerland, I was preaching in London when I received an invitation to go to Kuwait. I agreed to go, but during the trip there was an overnight layover, and I had to spend an entire day in the airport. As the day wore on, I felt more and more dejected. There was no shower room or changing room in the airport, and the only restaurant was outrageously expensive. I only had a little bit of food with me, and as I considered my dilemma, doubts filled my head: *Am I even in God's will? Why would God detain me for so long in an Arab airport?*

We finally got a flight and landed the next day. As I was walking toward customs, someone came running up from behind, asking, "Are you Brother PG Vargis?"

"Yes, I am PG Vargis."

"I am the senior airport officer. Here, give me your suitcase and bag and come with me at once," he commanded. He then whisked me past customs and out of the airport.

As it turned out, he knew of me. When I told him about my delayed flight, he said, "If you had arrived earlier, I wouldn't have been here."

What I didn't know before I spoke with him was that the cassettes, books, and Bibles in Hindi and English that I was carrying would never have been allowed into the country. Truly, God's timing is perfect. Sometimes even delays can be God's blessing.

During that same trip, I had prayed and asked God to supply the money for my airfare. That night as I prepared to preach, a brother suggested that I talk about my ministry. He told me that when the people's hearts were stirred, he would take up an offering for me.

I declined his offer, even though earlier that day I had received a letter from Lilly saying there was no money to pay the team or the children's school fees. She hadn't wanted me to worry—just to be aware of the situation. I was tempted to speak about the efforts of our team and challenge people to give to the Lord's work, but the reason I didn't was that I had learned a hard lesson a few years earlier. At another brother's similar request, I had spoken about our work in North India, and when the offering was received, it was a pittance. The Lord then reminded me that my job was preaching the gospel, not raising money...and that if I did my job, He would do His, and meet my needs.

So I didn't speak about our work that night—I knew that God would answer my prayer at the time and place of His choosing.

What I didn't know at the time was that the organizers of the meeting had already taken an offering on their own. I later learned it was the largest single offering they had ever collected in Kuwait up until that time.

But then came another challenge. In addition to the first offering, several others handed me cash and checks. Since they couldn't write the name of a Christian organization on the checks, they had made them out to me personally. I knew all the money was intended for the ministry and not my personal use, yet I was tempted to send one or two of the checks to Lilly to cover the children's school fees. However, we had agreed early on that any money we received would go to the team unless it clearly specified that it was for our personal use; besides, I had already written to Lilly that all the money I had received that day was for the team.

In the end, I refused the devil's lure and resolved to wait on the Lord.

The next day, a brother and his family came to meet with me. The man and his wife reminded me that they had been childless for many years and that I had prayed for them a couple of years earlier. With great excitement, they told me how the Lord had blessed them with a child the following year. They then handed me an envelope that contained local currency and said, "This is a gift for your children."

The Lord knows our hearts, and He opens up His treasuries to bless us. When I do His work, He takes care of me—and not just me but my family as well. Over and over, God taught me the lessons of His faithful provision in every aspect of our lives. When I am faithful in the little things, He entrusts me with more. Praise be to God!

In the early days, our only steady income, though small, came from the Christian books and gospels I was able to sell. If the weather was bad and I couldn't go out, there was no money. Many days we were hungry, but we learned that the God we serve is a prayer-hearing, prayer-answering God. The God of Elijah sent His ravens to feed us.

Not only did God faithfully provide for our physical needs, but also He began sending people to work with us. One of the first to come was a man who promised he would work for nothing. But one day God spoke to me and said, "You need to pay him fifty rupees every month."

When you have no money, paying someone even a small amount seems formidable! Nevertheless, I told him what God had said to me.

When I told Lilly, she was a little unnerved because she knew the state of our finances, or lack thereof.

After a few months, another brother resigned his job and joined us. We gave him half of the rice, wheat, flour, and sugar that the church gave us, but we had no money to pay him with.

That same week, we received a letter from a brother in the United Arab Emirates, asking us to recommend an evangelist they could support. We gave them our brother's name, and they began supporting him every month.

As the team grew, so did the support, and I realized the truth of what Hudson Taylor once said, "If you do the Lord's work according to His will, you will never lack His support."

It is when we step forward in faith that the waters part. If you stand at the shore waiting for them to part before taking a step, nothing will happen.

A Little Leaven Spoils the Whole Loaf

When the team was seventeen members strong, the support mysteriously began to dwindle. We prayed, but the situation did not improve. The lack of finances became so critical that many of the team members didn't even have enough money to pay their rent.

Meanwhile, we had been having some problems with one of the team members. His conduct was not consistent with that of a servant of God, and even though a few suggested that we extend a measure of compromise to him, we obeyed the voice of the Holy Spirit and released him. The next month the support increased.

Two weeks later we found out that he was involved in an adulterous affair. It wasn't a rumor—he had been caught red-handed. The Lord showed me that the sin of an evangelist stops the flow of blessing and provision.

There were several other times when the support for our ministry hit rock bottom, and on each occasion, prayer and careful inquiry disclosed team members who had not been honest with me about their motives and commitment to God's work. In each case, when those people had been dismissed from the team, our financial support returned, and we could fully supply the support for our remaining team members and cover the other needs of the ministry as well.

The lesson was clear: a dead fly putrefies even the finest perfume. I had to learn the lesson more than once that it's crucial not to be in a rush when hiring team members . . . but to scrutinize them carefully to determine their character.

STEPPING OUT: GOD'S HEAVENLY SUPPORT

As I mentioned, God taught me the truth of Hudson Taylor's words, "If you do the Lord's work according to His will, you will never lack His support." For IET, the word *support* has carried dual meaning—each time God compelled us to step out in faith, the support (resources, provision) we needed always showed up to support (sustain, or uphold) the assignment.

Can you relate? Hebrews 11:1 "supports" this kingdom principle: *Now faith is the substance of things hoped for, the evidence of things not seen* (NKJV). According to this verse, *faith* is two things, "substance" and "evidence":

- First, faith *is* substance. Your belief *is* actual matter, or material. When you step out in faith, you're not stepping onto thin air; you're stepping onto an actual *spiritual substance* that will hold you up.

- Second, faith *is* evidence. In legal terms, evidence is the *verifiable proof* that supports a person's testimony. Likewise, in biblical terms, faith is the *verifiable proof* that supports God's testimony, His Word. The very fact that you have faith *is* your proof that His promise will come to pass. Faith is a *knowing* deep within—you "know that you know that you know" God has said it. That He'll do it. You don't have tangible support in the natural realm yet, but the heavenly supply is already there, and the *unshakeable belief* God has planted in you is *evidence* that supports the soon physical appearance of that supply.

With these definitions in mind, you could personalize Hebrews 11:1 as follows: "My belief in God's promise to me is an actual spiritual substance that I'm standing on, and it's holding me up. I expect that spiritual substance to manifest in the natural realm anytime now, so that I can carry out my full assignment. My conviction that what God says is the absolute truth, supports me in every way. In fact, that deep-seated belief is all the proof I need to convince me that anything essential to carrying out His call *is* going to show up."

Step out in faith today! You can be sure that when you do, the Supporter of heaven and earth will send His heavenly supply to support His kingdom purposes that fulfill your earthly call.

> *Heavenly Father, I step out in faith today and stand on Your Word. You've promised to support me as I answer Your call. I choose to believe Romans 4:21, that "what You have promised, that You will do." Your support is all I need! I stand in faith, believing, and pray in Jesus' name. Amen.*

Chapter 10

THE ADVENTURE CONTINUES

Now to Him who is able to establish you according
to . . . the preaching of Jesus Christ . . .
—Romans 16:25

"WE MUST MOVE FROM PATHANKOT BEFORE ALL THE buildings are finished, so we don't become distracted and fix our minds on worldly things," Lilly said one day as we were enjoying dinner together.

Though I understood my wife's concern, I said, "Not until we finish these projects in North India and see them firmly established. Afterward we can move to another state."

We had felt for some time that we would be moving soon and were fairly certain we would be going somewhere else in northern India, perhaps Orissa or Bhopal. Orissa is a lush and beautiful region, a land of the aborigines, Satan-worship, poverty, immorality, and horrible skin diseases, so taking the gospel to this region seemed essential.

Meanwhile, the political turmoil in Punjab, with its bus and train strikes, meant that ministry there would be adversely affected because it was becoming increasingly difficult for people to get from one place to another. The IET headquarters was in Pathankot, and when the brothers had to journey there from other states, the killings and road strikes made their travels quite difficult. For that reason, we felt it was necessary to move our headquarters to another state.

Ultimately, we felt the Lord leading the work to Delhi, and we decided to open an office there. Neither Lilly nor I liked Delhi, so we began making arrangements to send someone else to oversee the expansion. The more I thought about it, however, the more I realized that we couldn't send someone else. At last, we decided to shift the main office to Delhi, and we realized that we would have to move there ourselves.

It was a much more difficult decision than it might have seemed on the surface because, years earlier, Lilly had undergone a horrible experience in Delhi that caused her to decide she would never live there again. We also had our five children to think about. In Pathankot, there was lots of room for them to play. We had a garden and plenty of fruit trees as well as various pets. There would be room for none of these things in a rented house in Delhi.

As for me, I like the rural agricultural life of the villages and have no affinity for the constraints of a large city and a bustling population. I love having the freedom to enjoy the beauty of nature and to worship and praise God aloud in His creation!

We had spacious accommodations and an abundance of room where we were, and the quiet atmosphere allowed me to write books and articles for the *Missionary Messenger* newsletter. In the gardens, I could refresh myself after a busy day, and the bounty from the fruit trees allowed us to share generously with others. We also enjoyed a certain level of status and respect among the people, and were invited to weddings, house dedications, the laying of foundation stones, and prayer meetings. Even the Hindus invited me to pray. Who in his right mind would want to leave all of that to move to a two-room house in Delhi where we knew no one?

Nonetheless, we had been in Pathankot for nine years, and the cloud had moved. It was time to follow it—even if it meant going to a place that offered none of the comforts we enjoyed.

In the first *Missionary Messenger* after our move to Delhi, I shared with our supporters the following:

> Greetings and love from Delhi, in the name of Jesus, who meets us, encourages us, consoles us, and exhorts us along the way!
>
> In the gospel of Mark, we read in several passages that when Jesus sent out His disciples, He went along with them. During these times, He corrected and consoled them (8:27; 8:33; 10:33). Mark also records that He often turned back and looked at the disciples.
>
> In our Christian journey, Jesus often turns back and looks at us, correcting, consoling, and exhorting us, because He cares about us.
>
> I recently had "an opportunity to look back" that I want to share with you.
>
> In Pathankot, we lived in a five-room house with a basement office, which the team leaders had built for our family. We never thought of leaving there until September 1985, when a move came up for consideration again. We were convinced this move was of the Lord. Even those who had at first resisted the idea were now encouraging us to move.
>
> So as the Lord confirmed His plans to us, we decided to go to Delhi, knowing that He was sending us there. Then, suddenly our children couldn't get admission into schools, and we couldn't find a suitable house. But because God had confirmed that we must move there, even though school admission was difficult for our children

and no one wanted to give a house to a person who did not have a job or permanent income, we remained determined—we would go even if our children lost an academic year and even if we had to live in a railway station for a few days. Because we were in God's will, it wasn't difficult to say good-bye to Pathankot. It was as easy as leaving a hotel room after a stay of several days.

When our brothers in the Evangelist's Bible College wept and embraced me as we said good-bye, I wasn't upset about leaving. The church congregation and workers in the compound came to say good-bye. Our typist burst into tears. Many of them told us we were leaving after making a garden out of barren land. Even the ripe fruit hanging from the trees, always a delightful treat, was not enough to tempt me to stay.

In April, Lilly and I and our children left for New Delhi. Pathankot was a wonderful place. We had good facilities, and people were friendly and courteous. Yet it was not a problem to leave because our hearts were not attached to those things.

I went back into my vacant office and looked around. I had spent a lot of time there, praying often and asking many things of God. I reflected on the past fifteen years—fourteen in the Lord's service, eleven of which were spent as the leader of evangelists.

I looked at my life from the day I was saved and examined it from all sides. I had placed my heart at His feet and said many things.

I was saved in 1971 and became a servant of the Lord in 1972. As I looked back, I was aware of many mistakes I had made in my life, some of them serious. I confessed them before the Lord. Sometimes I have behaved unjustly with my wife and children. I asked them for their forgiveness.

In the fourteen years I have served the Lord, He has blessed me greatly, and I thank God for that. The growth of the Team has been impressive, provoking some to envy. Having started without resources, the Lord has lifted us to great heights! I am indeed blessed to have an excellent team of coworkers. He has given me people to love and care for. O God, how great Thou art!

How many hundreds of thousands of rupees have passed through my hands, spent for the extension of His kingdom?! How many church halls were built?! Hundreds of evangelists were given bicycles, and a few were given scooters. Orphans were taken care of in three orphanages.

When I look back, I thank God that my hands are clean and I have no guilt. I spent all He gave me for His work. From out of His provision for my family, I spent a part of it on gospel work. By His grace, neither my heart nor my hands are stained by money.

I wanted to distribute tracts, not be a leader, but God made me a leader of a diverse group of people who speak many different languages. He made me a leader of the fastest growing missionary movement in India, which has baptized the largest number of people. As I look back, I see my mistakes in recruiting some I shouldn't have, but I was never guilty of misusing the authority vested in me. Even when I dealt with those who worked against me, I acted as a servant of God. It was all by God's grace. Praise be to God.

I am forty-eight years old. I promised God I wouldn't repeat my past mistakes and would work more earnestly.

Many people came to tell us good-bye. Some were crying. There were believers and non-believers, Christians and non-Christians. I said good-bye to everyone and everything. Lilly was emotional. It was difficult for her to leave the people she loved so much.

I looked around again at the place we were bidding farewell. A Bible school, good buildings, good land, and beautiful flowers. I was so happy that God had used me to bring about all these things that I shed tears of joy and gratitude.

As I was getting into the van, I saw the trees with their ripe fruit. Someone said, "Brother Vargis planted them all, but he is leaving before enjoying the fruit." It was true, but the fruits of my labor I will gather in the Promised Land.

Well-wishers poured into the railway station. Many of my little Timothys were crying like babies as the train pulled out of the station.

We arrived in Delhi on April 15, and began adjusting to our two-room flat, which would serve as both our home and office.

It was very hot. At night we slept in the courtyard. Mercifully, the mosquitoes weren't too bad.

We had come to a new place with new resolutions. The Lord who consoled the disciples would console us. The Lord who walked with the two on the road to Emmaus would walk with us as well.

As I write this today, I know Jesus will walk with me through my life's journey and bring me safely to the other shore. While He hung from the cross, Jesus entrusted His mother to His beloved disciple John. That same Savior will take care of me and my wife and children. May the same God bless you and grant you His peace.

God's blessings are reserved for His children. The many letters that land on my desk proclaim the miracle of answered prayer. The unemployed are employed, the sick are healed, sinners are convicted, the childless are blessed with children. It is by God's grace that this ministry grew, but it was your prayers that moved the hand of God. Praise be to God. And we thank you for your prayers.

I am happy and content as I write these lines. I have no regrets. What a blessing it was that I could resign my job and follow the Lord.

We live in a two-room house. One is our bedroom and the other is our office. There are no tables or chairs other than a stool for the typist. A suitcase on a cot becomes the table.

But we are enthusiastic about the Lord's work! I can travel much more easily, and it is easier for others to come meet me.

If statesmen felt New Delhi should be the capital of India, evangelists, too, must make it their capital for the kingdom of God in India.

It is for God to decide how long we should stay here. When the cloud moves again, we will move too, without complaint or hesitation. When the cloud stops, we will pitch our tent.

Looking back, I realize I am not worthy of all this. His abounding grace wrought much through me. Looking ahead, I see expenses and responsibility for five hundred evangelists in ten states. Yet as Lilly said, "The Lord has helped us 'til now and this same God will help us again."

Our journey continued.

STEPPING OUT: GOD'S HEAVENLY SUPPLY

Have you ever wanted to step out and obey God, but you wonder how God's heavenly supply will manifest in the natural realm? Second Corinthians 4:18 says to fix your eyes on the unseen, or eternal, not on what is seen, or temporary. And Romans 4:17 teaches that you must call into being the things that don't yet exist in this realm.

God is the great I AM. He not only knows the past; He's already lived out the future. According to Isaiah 46:10, at the beginning of time, He declared the end. So when you fix your eyes on the eternal—the promises in the Word that God has given you specifically about your situation—you're aligning your heart with the future He's already seen. Then, as you begin to declare those promises out loud, you "call into being" the things that haven't manifested yet. In so doing, you release God's kingdom supply into this earthly realm.

In the kingdom of heaven, there's no sin, sickness, or bondage. No poverty, fear, or grief. There's only peace, wholeness, and joy. There is righteousness, health, and protection. When you pray, "Father, Your kingdom come; Your will be done," you're releasing His heavenly supply into your situation. Don't get the wrong idea—it's not a magic formula. But the more you read the Word and pray, the more you'll see with "eyes of understanding" the kingdom supply God says is yours. And the more you step out and declare His promises in faith, the sooner that supply will manifest.

What compels you today? Has God asked you to step out in faith, but you need peace of mind? Do you need healing? God's protection? The salvation of your entire household or a harvest of souls in your community? No matter the issue, step out in faith. Fix your eyes on His eternal Word, and call His promises into being. God's abundant, heavenly supply is yours, just waiting for the taking!

The following are just a few of His eternal promises that you can fix your eyes and heart on, and call into being in your life.

- For forgiveness:

    I confess my sin, and You are faithful and righteous to forgive my sin and to cleanse me from all unrighteousness (1 John 1:9).

- For healing, whether emotional, mental, physical, or relational:

    Jesus, You bore my sins in Your body on the cross, that I might die to sin and live to righteousness; for by Your wounds I was healed (1 Peter 2:24).

- For peace of mind and freedom from worry:

    I am anxious for nothing, but in everything by prayer and supplication with thanksgiving I let my requests be made known to You, God. And Your peace, which surpasses all comprehension, guards my heart and my mind in Christ Jesus (Philippians 4:6–7).

- For victory over strongholds and temptations:

    No temptation has overtaken me but such as is common to man; and, God, You are faithful, who will not allow me to be tempted beyond what I am able, but with the temptation will provide the way of escape also, that I may be able to endure it (1 Corinthians 10:13).

- For the salvation of your loved ones and reaching others who are lost:

I thank You that just as Cornelius and his whole household were saved, Lydia and her whole household were baptized, and the jailor and his entire household were saved, so my loved ones and my whole household will be saved. (See Acts 10:9–11:18; 16:15; 16:25–35.)

Lord of the harvest, send workers into Your harvest field (Matthew 9:32) to reach my loved ones and the lost of my community.

Chapter 11

THE BOUNTIFUL
BLESSINGS OF GOD

Now to Him who is able to do exceeding abundantly
above all that we ask or think...
—Ephesians 3:20

IN FEBRUARY 1981, PASTOR JOHN OSTEEN, FROM THE UNITED STATES, called and said he would like to meet me. His flight was coming in the next day, and he was hoping I could take the time for us to spend a few days together.

I dressed the best I could and went to meet him at the airport. When Pastor Osteen and a friend arrived, another Indian pastor who had scheduled meetings for them also came to greet them. After greetings and introductions, Pastor Osteen asked me to share my testimony, and then he had a lot of questions for me. After answering his questions and telling him about our work, the four of us left to visit some of our mission churches. When we visited Katra, I spotted one of our believers working, even though it was pouring rain. I stopped the car and said, "Tell everyone I am here. If they can come at two o'clock, we can pray for a while, and I will be able to meet with them."

The Indian pastor translated this for Pastor Osteen, and then added, "No one will come in this cold rain." I had worked for years with the believers of Katra, and knowing them very well, I was certain they would come. Sure enough, around one thirty that afternoon, they came trickling in. Over thirty of them had braved the bitter cold to come.

The people sat on the floor while I stood. There, drenched in rain and shivering from the cold, they began clapping their hands and singing praises to God. I witnessed one of the greatest outpourings of the Holy Spirit I had ever seen. The power of God was unbelievable!

I asked Pastor Osteen to preach, but he declined because the presence of the Holy Ghost was so awesome that people were on their feet, praising the Lord.

The next Sunday John Osteen came to our church in Jammu, and sixty-five people came, including a man whom the Lord healed of a paralytic stroke after I prayed for him.

Then Pastor Osteen visited Pathankot, where he stayed in the government guesthouse and had dinner with us. After dinner we went to the prayer room, and I told him all about the work of the team. The next day as we headed to visit with the team, we stopped by the land we had bought, and I explained our plans.

As we looked over the land, Pastor Osteen said, "Buy the entire plot. You will need it when the work expands."

"No," I replied, "we only need the high places. If the Lord provides even half of it, that would be a great gift."

Later, after the team meeting, Pastor Osteen asked Lilly and me to stay behind because he said he had something he wanted to share with us.

When everyone else had left, he put his hands on our shoulders and said, "You are my children. Lilly is my daughter and Vargis is my son. I have seen how you live and sleep, and I want you to know that you don't have to suffer like this. You don't have to sleep on the floor in a rented house or ride an old bicycle anymore. I came here because Jesus spoke to me. I want to give you a gift. It is not from my church. It's a gift from the Osteen family to the Vargis family. I personally want to give you one hundred thousand dollars, in addition to a gift from our church."

I was very surprised and grateful, and it was a few moments before I could speak. Finally I said, "Pastor Osteen, I thank you for the gift, which is far beyond anything I could dream of, but I can't receive it in my name or in my family's name. We vowed that we would never amass wealth. If you give me the gift, I will buy the land in the name of our team, build the Bible school, and make it our headquarters."

Pastor Osteen again expressed his desire to make my family more comfortable while we worked for the Lord, and again I had to decline. After a long silence, Pastor Osteen said, "I will send it to your family. You can do with it as you please."

John Osteen returned to the United States and sent the money to us. With it, I bought three and a half acres in the name of our team and built the Bible school.

Thus, what could be called a personal loss for me became great gain for God's kingdom. Many are the evangelists who have come out of the Bible school and are now working all over North India. Truly, the Lord is my portion. Serving Him has been the greatest joy of my life, even during the dark times of persecution.

ENDURING PERSECUTION

Angry because of all that was being accomplished through IET, the devil put into motion a plan intended to destroy the integrity of our mission. Rumors and false accusations that I had inappropriately used money sent in by supporters and that one of the ministry properties was registered in my name began to spread. Even though that was not the case and could easily be verified and substantiated by bank statements, property documents, and other financial records, I was very troubled. I knew that in addition to causing my own pain and suffering, these totally unfounded rumors could cause distrust in our supporters and turmoil within our team. That is exactly what happened.

The devil had a field day. Financial support began to dwindle, and vicious lies continued to circulate. The devil whispered in my ear, "Vargis, your team is going to split. All your efforts and hard work have been in vain."

Heartsick about the state of events, I went to a convention with my family, and together, we laid everything before the Lord. As we worshipped there, the Lord ministered His grace to me, and the anguish lifted.

By that time, many of our team members had left, and we were facing a financial crisis. I called the remaining team leaders to Delhi and filled them in on the situation. I suggested that perhaps we should join another mission team, but they would have none of it. "We will wait upon the Lord. Even if all the financial support dries up, we will not leave this organization to join another one."

GOD'S FAITHFULNESS PREVAILS

With that decision made, we moved forward with faith in our miracle-working God—and He did not disappoint us. Gradually the financial support of the ministry began to increase, and He called and equipped many other qualified people to become a part of IET. I was blessed to have a fine group of solid leaders who had a vision of faith for all that God wanted to accomplish through IET. Truly these men and women—people who have a hunger and thirst for righteousness—heeded Jesus' council in Matthew 6:20: *"Lay up for yourselves treasures in heaven, where neither moth nor rust destroys."* Someday in heaven, these devoted workers will be rewarded in full for their faithfulness.

I learned a lot through the times of testing. I realized that the success of a ministry does not depend on money but on God's grace alone. God also taught me not to get upset when expected support stops, but to always display the integrity befitting a servant of the Lord.

Time proved my true character. God honored and vindicated me, and today I am honored in the nation for my integrity.

PATIENCE AND TRANSFORMING POWER

If you've been walking with God for any length of time, you've probably experienced some sort of trial. The way you respond when you're under attack speaks volumes about the level of God's grace and power at work in your life: Will you stand strong in Him and walk in the Spirit no matter what? Or will you give in to the enemy and resort to walking in the flesh?

James 1:2–4 provides essential information on how to act during a trial: *Dear brothers and sisters, whenever trouble comes your way, let it be an opportunity for joy. For when your faith is tested, your endurance has a chance to grow. So let it grow, for when your endurance is fully developed, you will be strong in character and ready for anything* (NLT).

Here are some dos and don'ts to remember during times of trial:

- ⊘ Don't let your emotions rule you.
  - ✔ Do press into His presence and walk in the Spirit.
- ⊘ Don't doubt God's ability or His concern.
  - ✔ Do ask for wisdom and expect Him to give it.
- ⊘ Don't focus on the circumstances.
  - ✔ Do pray that God's will would be done.

⊘ Don't jump ship.
  ✔ Do remain faithful in the faith.
⊘ Don't grow impatient.
  ✔ Do let endurance develop to full maturity.
⊘ Don't take revenge against people.
  ✔ Do remember who the real enemy is.
⊘ Don't give in to discouragement or bitterness.
  ✔ Do rejoice! The battle is His; the victory is sure.

One last thing—during a trial, the enemy may tempt you to define yourself apart from who you really are: "Everybody says I'm this," or "I guess I'll always be like that." Don't buy into it! Remember who you are *in Christ.* As 2 Corinthians 13:4 teaches, even though you are weak, you *live in Him and have God's power* (NLT).

The word *power* is the Greek word *dunamis,* also where we get our word *dynamite.* Just picture the explosive, "dynamite" power that raised Jesus Christ from the dead. That same power still fills Him today. Now picture your life *in Him*—and that Holy Ghost, resurrection power at work *in you* and your situation. His power will raise you above the most besetting of circumstances.

The next time the enemy brings trouble your way and you feel like giving in to weakness, stop! Tell yourself, "I refuse to give in. I live *in Him,* and His resurrection power is at work *in me.*" Then be patient...and rejoice! The testing of your faith is producing an endurance that will leave you *strong in character and ready for anything*!

> *Praise You, Father! Your power is at work in me, helping me endure the trials I face and building the character of Jesus in me. I rejoice to know that You are perfecting patience in me! I purpose to let patience have its complete work, that I might be mature in You, ready for Your call. In Jesus' name, I pray. Amen.*

Chapter 12

EQUIPPING THE CALLED

"Oh that Thou wouldst bless me indeed, and enlarge
my border, and that Thy hand might be with me."
—1 Chronicles 4:10

As the graduates of the Bible school began going into the mission field two by two and planting churches, I did everything I could to teach them from my heart. I shared my notes and sermons with them, and we talked constantly about the character and power of the Holy Spirit and the work He was accomplishing in our lives and the ministry.

I did my best to teach them that without the Holy Spirit nothing could be accomplished—certainly nothing of lasting kingdom value—but that with the Holy Spirit anything was possible. I began the practice of traveling to each state once a year to work with and encourage pastors, leaders, and workers. I continue this practice today. While I am there, I listen to their stories and their problems and give them advice. Like a father to young sons, I teach them how to pray for the sick, how to touch and communicate with people, and how to take part in the lives of those they're ministering to.

IET makes sure these men and women of God have enough literature, gospel tracts, New Testaments, and Bibles for their work. As provision comes in, IET tries to give the pastors a bicycle within the first year of their work and, if possible, to provide the leader with a motorbike. It is imperative that they have the tools they need to carry out the work in their areas. Now that the Lord has opened the doors for making films, the leaders of each state need jeeps to transport film and equipment to the various evangelical outreaches.

Media Opportunities

My passion, my life's work, my vision, and my calling are for the lost souls of India. Not a single day goes by that I'm not somewhere preaching and teaching about the marvelous gift of salvation that comes through Jesus Christ.

My heart has always been for those who have not yet heard the good news. In the '80s, I had a deep desire to preach on Trans World Radio, a media outlet that had tremendous potential to reach souls with the gospel. One believer graciously paid for a season's broadcast time, but the director objected to my praying for the sick and would not allow me to be on the air.

Of course, I was surprised by this reaction and disappointed that the door of opportunity seemed to be closed. Nonetheless, I spoke my conscience. "Even if you offered to let me preach every day in every language, I would rather preach in the streets and bazaars than to stop praying for the sick," I replied.

As soon as I'd finished the sentence, I felt the Lord pat me on the shoulder.

Later, while I was on a preaching tour in Kuwait, a brother who had been saved during a radio broadcast asked, "Vargis, why aren't you on the radio?"

When I explained the unfortunate encounter with Trans World Radio, he immediately bought a year's worth of radio time on Radio Ceylon—a secular station. Thus began a weekly radio program that was established in 1988.

TELEVISION BECOMES A TOOL

Today, the number of television sets sold in India and the availability of channels continue to skyrocket. There are hundreds of channels in various languages, with many more being added all the time. But in 1988, there was only one Christian station. Although I knew television could reach as vast an audience as the radio messages could—and with better results—I had never pursued it. Buying television time seemed too expensive to be justified, so I never even prayed about it. I had somewhat of a desire to be on television, but only from the standpoint of being able to communicate with people. God had trained me to be a communicator, and it was a job He has taught me to do well. Still, at that point, buying air time seemed out of the question.

God had other plans, however. Joy Thomas, the man who eventually became the second president of IET, suggested that it would be a good idea to look into the possibility. He spoke to a brother in our media department, and things began to come together quickly.

Finally the question was not whether to buy air time, but whether to be on one of the non-Christian channels or the Christian channel. I felt sure that it should be the non-Christian channel because our goal has always been to reach the lost. Consequently, we bought a thirty-minute time slot that would air our program at six o'clock in the morning. Then,

Then, in order to save money, we rented a hall where I recorded twenty-six messages in two days.

I decided that rather than preaching to the audience, I would simply talk to them about the things Jesus wanted to do in their lives. I explained that what He would do for one, He would do for all, whether it be a husband, wife, student, teacher, or businessman. I challenged the listeners—regardless of who they were or where they lived—to fly higher with Jesus. I appealed to them not to change the channel, saying, "Give me twenty-two minutes of your time, and your life will never be the same."

My message was—and is—that Jesus is waiting and ready to help anyone with any area of need. Whether it's salvation, healing, family problems, finances, health, or business issues, Jesus is the solution. My goal has always been to make the message so appealing that every listener will be eager to pick up a Bible and learn more about how to become a Christian.

The programs have been very popular, in part because we present teaching that is very different from anything the people have heard before. For example, India has no teaching about the practical matters of family life, so when I tell the viewers that the Bible is full of instructions on how we should live each day, it is appealing to them. Even the station manager is surprised at how well the viewers are receiving the messages. But I'm not. God's heart beats for the people of India.

God has opened the doors for me to preach on two channels—one in Malayalam and one in which the message, given in English, is translated into Hindi. Now that God has opened our eyes to the potential and opportunities, we are praying for the needed finances to broadcast to the other ten language groups where we have outreaches and evangelical meetings. My heart is that these people also have the opportunity to be encouraged by practical lessons of faith, holiness, and victorious living.

Television has proven to be the most effective means for reaching the upper caste. When we go into the villages to preach the gospel, only the lower-caste people come to hear us. A Brahman, upper caste, or wealthy person won't come to the meetings with lower-caste people. The beautiful thing about television is that they don't have to! We can reach them in their own living rooms with the good news of the gospel.

Every week I get hundreds of letters and phone calls from these upper-caste people, wanting to know more and asking for help with various problems in their lives. We praise God for allowing us to minister on television—it has truly been the means for our growing success in reaching this segment of the population.

Our prayer is that the Church will become strong and that more people from the upper caste and business sector will become Christians, because that can change the nation. Right now most Christians are from the lower castes and don't have a voice in government. But as God opens the doors for additional television opportunities, the groundwork can be laid for tremendous change. It's an exciting thought.

BREAKING BARRIERS

It's quite possible that I am the first Christian leader to talk about family life in India. Even now there's not much teaching available on the subject. I wrote a book on marriage and began talking to my pastors and leaders about their roles in the family—about the godly way to care for their wives and children. This made many of them uncomfortable at first, because in the Indian culture, any reference to your wife is considered sexual. But I knew that I had an obligation to God to teach the truth of His Word, which has plenty to say about families, wives, and children. I had to be willing to break the barriers.

In India, men and women sit on opposite sides of the church, so I began to ask the men to sit with their wives and hold their hands while I prayed for the family. This was very difficult for them, and though their reluctance was hard to overcome, changes have gradually occurred.

I also taught about the need for women to be treated with respect— a real departure from Indian culture. There is a saying in India that it is better to be born dirt than to be born a girl. Women are generally kept behind the scenes and are not involved in decision-making. But I encouraged the men to talk things over with their wives and to eat with their families. These were radical concepts, but the gospel can set the captives free and change the way people think.

People began calling me a "wife worshipper" and asked why I opened the car door for my wife. They accused me of behaving like the Americans! So I took the matter before the Lord, and He showed me a passage where Moses helped his wife and children get on their donkeys. The next week I preached from that verse, and told the people that the donkey was Moses' car, and if he was helping his wife and children four thousand years ago, we should be doing the same now.

Many times God gave me specific Bible verses with which to encourage the pastors and various congregations. I began writing about these things in magazines and books, and began teaching them on the television program. Some of the older folks are still resistant to these ideas because they are so radically different from what they were taught growing up, but the young people are latching onto them and many spouses are beginning to hold hands with each other in church when we sing and pray.

It is my constant prayer that God will raise up more preachers to talk about family life so that the Christian families will provide a stark contrast to non-Christian homes.

Making Movies for Jesus

When I was in our first mission station in Katra, a very old woman came to work with us for a couple of weeks. She had an 8mm movie projector and a film about Jesus. She and the man she worked with showed the first part of the movie, and then she climbed on a table or chair and preached. Next they played the second half of the movie with the sound off and told the story of the crucifixion as it unfolded on the screen behind her. I saw the power of such a tool because it broke through the strict social barriers in a way that nothing else ever had. Everyone—the upper caste, lower caste, educated, and illiterate—sat together spellbound as they listened to the message of the gospel. Movies provided unprecedented interaction between factions that virtually never crossed social lines.

When Pastor John Osteen gave us a gift of half a million dollars, I felt as if God were shaking my hand. Certainly, He was empowering His work to expand, because I was able to buy all the equipment we needed for the next two years. Not a penny went into my pocket, not even for the office. All the money was spent for the mission field. I bought all the Bibles and bicycles that were needed at that time, as well as forty-five motorbikes and thirteen jeeps. I wrote a letter to Campus Crusade and told them that IET had been given the means to buy thirteen jeeps. I also asked if they could provide thirteen movie projectors. They agreed, so I wrote to Dayspring International, informing them that we had been given thirteen movie projectors and asking if they could donate thirteen copies of the Indian version of the *Jesus* film.

Unbeknownst to me, Director John Gilman, a Dayspring representative, was in India at the time of my request. His wife called him from America and said, "PG Vargis needs thirteen copies of the Indian version of the *Jesus* film." Thirty minutes later, the man walked into my office and agreed to send the films.

The Lord has faithfully used these precious gifts to spread the gospel message across India, but the need for resources is ever-present and growing.

The idea to make movies of our own was born when I saw a movie called *Prodigal*, which was produced by the Billy Graham Evangelical Association. While I was watching it, I thought, *Someone needs to produce a movie like this for India.*

In January 2002, while I was sitting on the platform at a crusade, the Lord gave me the storyline for a movie. I wrote the first five pages right there!

One year later, in January 2003, we released that movie, the first one ever produced by a Christian minister in India. The film, which tells the story of a prodigal father, was very well received by the masses. Many missions are using it as a tool to reach the affluent and educated.

So far we have made two movies, and a third is in the works. While the first movie is geared toward the wealthier class of society, the second is directed toward the common man. The second movie is far better than the first because it includes many important messages: salvation, forgiveness, helping one's neighbor, the power of prayer, and the necessity of faith. Our third movie, soon to be released, focuses on healing.

These movies have proven to be effective tools for preparing the hearts of people to hear the gospel. We show the movie and then preach the message of salvation afterward. Several evangelical missions and churches are also showing these films. One large church in Kerala shows a movie every week, using it to attract non-Christians to the church where they can hear the plan of salvation explained.

We are mass-producing VCDs of these films to hand out to people, and we give a copy of the New Testament to individuals who come to us with questions after seeing the movie. We also give a copy of the entire Bible to anyone who comes to a saving knowledge of the Lord Jesus Christ.

What a blessing it has been to see God's truth as it spreads across India and to witness those whose lives are changed not only through preaching but also through the use of Christian movies, Bibles, and New Testaments.

Equipped with Every Good Thing

Whether your passion lies in taking the gospel to your neighborhood or to the other side of town, across your country or to a foreign field on the other side of the world, it will require compelling faith for you to venture out. But the Lord will never send you unequipped. In fact, Hebrews

13:20–21 says that the *great Shepherd of the sheep* [will] *equip you with everything good for doing his will* (NIV).

Here are a few points to remember as you prepare to answer the call:

- Only go where you are called. The equipping goes with the appointment.
- Pray before setting out. No lasting work happens apart from Him (John 15:5), but with Him all things are possible (Mark 10:27). Pray that He will direct your steps (Proverbs 3:6), but don't try to analyze what He says—just step out in faith and obedience. Ask Him to send other laborers into the field, as well (Luke 10:2).
- Take authority over evil spirits. Jesus gave His disciples authority over all unclean spirits (Mark 6:7). He also told them to pray and fast when dealing with such spirits (Mark 9:28–29).
- When the setting is new or especially difficult, don't feel you have to "go it alone." Kingdom work is not often a solitary assignment. Jesus sent the disciples out two by two when they began, not one by one.
- Be prepared to stand strong in your convictions, should you meet resistance. As Jesus said in Mark 6:11, "If anyone won't receive you, 'shake off the dust!'"
- Partner with others. Don't be afraid to ask for financial help if you need it. God can bless you through those who work in the marketplace. Though they may not be able to answer the same calling, the Lord may compel them to support your work.

Remember, if Jesus sends you out, He'll be with you every step of the way. Not only that, but He'll supply you with every good thing you need. The Lord equips the called!

Father, I am so grateful that You called me. You could have used anyone, but You wanted me. My desire is to walk worthy of the call to advance Your kingdom. I place my trust in You and abandon my own wisdom. Should I ever begin to doubt that I won't have everything I need to finish my assignment, help me to remember that You equip those You call. You have workers and resources that I know nothing about, and I trust them to show up at the right time. I praise Your holy name. Amen.

Chapter 13

HOW GREAT THE NEED

"Thou wast slain, and didst purchase for God with Thy blood
men from every tribe and tongue and people and nation."
—Revelation 5:9

INDIA IS A VAST AND VARIED COUNTRY WITH MANY RELIGIONS, languages, customs, traditions, and influences. One sixth of the total world population—more than one billion people—live in India. Every year, the people of India add more to the world's population than any other country and are only the second people group after China to cross the one billion mark.

The country occupies only 2.4 percent of the world's land area, yet it supports over 15 percent of the world's population with 40 percent (or over 380 million), being younger than fifteen. Approximately 6,850 children under the age of five died today. Another 6,850 will die tomorrow and every day after that.

Over 50 percent of the population is illiterate. Recognizing that education is one of the keys to breaking the cycle of poverty, many of our missionaries provide adult literacy classes to parents. The free schools that IET has established allow us to help children whose parents are able to feed and clothe them but cannot afford to educate them.

While the government recognizes eighteen official languages, with Hindi and English being the most widely spoken, there are literally hundreds of dialects spoken throughout the country, and the need for missionaries to these language groups is critical.

The need for workers who understand India's various religions is also great. Eighty-three percent of the population is Hindu, and India has one of the largest Muslim populations in the world as well. In addition, India is home to Sikhs, Jains, Buddhists, and Parsis, who serve over 3.3 billion gods and goddesses. People from these religions desperately need to hear the life-changing message of salvation through the one true God, Jesus Christ.

Although the caste system, a confusing concept to most Westerners, was outlawed in 1949, it is still an important identification factor for most Hindus and a potent fact of political life as well. There are four broad categories of castes, with thousands of sub-castes within each major group. Despite economic modernization and laws against discrimination, the practice still exists. The "untouchables" represent one of the cruelest forms of discrimination ever inflicted on an entire people group. In an attempt to help remove their stigma and integrate them into Indian society, Ghandi renamed these people *Harijan*, which means "children of God." It was the children of these untouchables that Lilly and I taught in the early days in Katra.

Only the Truth Will Set Them Free

The needs are practical, to be sure, but even more than that, they are spiritual. India is a stranglehold of demonic activity and is steeped in spiritual deception. Christians are severely persecuted yet, as history shows, the

Church always falters in times of prosperity and thrives in times of persecution. Opposition has only made us stronger and more determined.

Interestingly, the greatest causes of famine and the many problems and diseases that come as a result, are not poor agricultural practices, poor political or economic policies, lack of science and technology, or even overpopulation. While all these things can and do add to the basic problem, the core issue is spiritual. Less than 15 percent of the land in the world that is suitable for cultivation is used for agriculture, and even then for only half the year. There is no major area of the world that, with proper, available technology, would not be able to support its own population and beyond.

The reality is that the countries in the world that don't have Christian roots invariably place a very low value on human life. For example, the poverty in India can quite fairly be laid at the feet of Hinduism and the other false religions it helped spawn. Hindu philosophy teaches that a human being is the incarnation of a soul that is on its way to *moksha,* a kind of final resting place. Reaching this destination may take countless, even unending cycles of reincarnation in both human and animal form. A person works his way to higher forms by doing good deeds and, likewise, falls to lower forms by sinning.

Poverty, disease, starvation, and the like are seen as divine punishments for which the person must do various kinds of penance in order to be reborn into a higher form the next time around. Offering help to individuals in poverty or any type of distress is seen as interfering with their karma, and thereby causing them spiritual harm. Obviously, such views are quite the opposite of biblical teaching about salvation, grace, mercy, and compassion.

In Hinduism, every animal is thought to be an incarnation of either people or deities. Cows are held in especially high esteem because they are believed to be incarnated deities, of which there are over 3.3 billion. Not only are cows not to be eaten for this reason, but they also contribute heavily to the food problem by consuming 20 percent of India's food supply. The same holds true for rats and mice, which eat 15 percent of the food supply and are not killed because they might be someone's reincarnated relative.

These deceptions make it difficult for the truth to penetrate the Hindu mindset. There is tremendous need for the "light of the gospel" of the one true God to dispel such staggering spiritual darkness and "set the captives free."

THE DAUGHTER-IN-LAW DILEMMA

Despite India's recent economic development—and quite possibly as a direct result of it—there are other problems as well. You can pick up newspapers anywhere in the world and read of the problems that plague this country I have given my life to serve.

For example, the practice of a bride's family giving a dowry to the groom's family is an old and established tradition that guarantees a bride wealth of her own, should something ever happen to her husband. Although this practice has been illegal since 1961, the law against it has actually added to the problem. The majority of Indian families still pay some form of dowry to seal their daughter's wedding agreements. But rather than having a public record of the dowry, as was done in the past, the dowry has become a negotiating point between families, and there are no records or receipts. The recent economic changes haven't changed the system—they have only made people greedier. The dowry has become a quick means to gain wealth and obtain the trophies of the middle-class. Marriage has been reduced from a sacred ceremony to a way to achieve status and material gain. Furthermore, demands for cash and gifts often continue long after the wedding has taken place. The lure of easy money crosses all levels of Indian society, whether rich or poor, educated or uneducated, marrying for love or by parental arrangement.

When trouble develops over a dowry payment, it's often deadly. Authorities tell tragic stories of brides being doused in kerosene and set on fire, locked in closets until they starve, and beaten in front of their husbands' families. Often the murders are disguised as suicides or kitchen accidents.

There is no word in Sanskrit (a language in India) for divorce and, thus, no way to dissolve a marriage. As a result, the horrible practice of wife-burning (so that the groom can find another bride and receive another dowry) is reaching epidemic proportions. The victims become ostracized and are left horribly disfigured, if in fact they survive at all.

The Church has been tragically silent about the issues of dowry because Christians are afraid of offending people. However, if nobody preaches against the practice, it won't change. Jesus said He came with a sword, and we at IET are doing our best, through our books, magazines, and TV programs, to teach the truth and lay an ax to the root of greed.

DESPERATE MEASURES

Poverty and false belief systems cause many people in India to make choices they would not normally make. These two factors also often work together to trigger desperation in their victims.

If a poor man comes on hard times and he happens to own two bulls, he can sell one or both to a wealthy man who is looking for such an opportunity; or, if a poor man has land or gold, he can sell it to meet his expenses. But many times, instead of selling the resource, a man who is poor will use it as collateral to receive a high-interest-rate loan. These emergency loans—called "blades" because they cut like a blade and bleed people dry—are so difficult to repay, that borrowers often despair of ever being able to do so, and as a result, they commit suicide.

The poor may also feel pressured to abort or sell their children. Female fetuses are often aborted because girls are viewed as burdens families must support and one day provide substantial dowries for. Consequently, the population of India is imbalanced, with men making up the higher percentage.

In March 2006, a newspaper reported that a couple in Orissa sold their eight-month-old daughter to another couple for eight hundred rupees ($20 US currency). The parents had eked out a living doing menial tasks, but following the birth of her daughter, the mother became ill and was hospitalized. When the couple couldn't pay the bill, they decided to sell their child. A couple (the parents of two sons) from a neighboring village bought her. Most likely she will become a servant in the household and will never marry.

While it is common for a girl to be sold as a servant to a wealthy household, boys are not exempt. A poor man who has a girl or a boy, six years or older in age, may feel he has no other choice but to pledge the child as a bond servant in exchange for needed money. Though the child can be released after the loan is paid back, this scenario rarely happens.

The belief that males are superior to females causes some parents to take matters into their own hands. It is common practice for the parents of a newborn girl to bribe hospital staff into switching their baby with a boy born on the same day. It is also not unusual for people to buy a boy when they don't have a male in the family. Oftentimes, they are driven to do this when the daughter-in-law is under such pressure from the son's family to produce a male heir that "purchasing a son" seems the only option. Such endeavors must be kept secret, of course, because if the grandparents discover that the child was bought and is not a blood relative, they will withhold any inheritance.

MORE PROBLEMS FOR GIRLS

It is a curse for women to give birth to girls. Not only do the girls receive less food than their brothers, the girls also do all the work. Suffering and servitude are their lot. There is a saying that a girl is never free. When she's young, she is her father's possession; when she marries, she is her husband's possession; and when she is old, she is the servant of her sons. If three or four girls are born into a family, it's a nightmare. Many are sold into prostitution.

Girls are often bought and sold like cattle. Usually a girl will be bought by a middleman who gives the family some money for her and then lies about the amount he was paid. The girl becomes the lifelong property of a matron and will be raped repeatedly to break her resistance. She then will be put to work in a brothel, and the matron will receive the lion's share of the money. If the girl has any children, they also will become the matron's property and will likely be used as prostitutes. The girls can't run away because there is nowhere for them to go. Once they have been violated, they know that no one will marry them, so they stay in the brothel because it gives them a place to live. They work until they die of AIDS or some other disease.

ORPHANS IN INDORE

In our children's home in Indore, there are sixty-two children whom we saved from poverty. They live in two halls with limited facilities. The children sleep on carpet strips laid over a concrete floor. But, thank God, their parents didn't sell them. They receive good food and attend school.

Somehow, thirty-two children squeeze themselves into one jeep for the five-mile ride to school. Don't ask me how they do it! The rest of the children are home-schooled. We are praying fervently, believing God for a school bus and another building that has adequate facilities, proper beds, a cooking house, and a dining hall.

In June 2006, Lilly came to take care of the children's home. We felt compelled to help with the orphanage and to begin a church-planting ministry in the area.

WINDS OF CHANGE

I am thankful that India is awakening to receive Jesus Christ. Though subtle, a sure and strong sound of people worshipping the true God now rises from every corner of India. And while persecution of Christians continues and even increases, people are being saved and pioneer churches are being planted in every state. Entire people groups that were once resistant and indifferent to the gospel are asking for preachers to come and share the good news with their tribes.

As a result of fervent prayer, God has opened previously locked doors in ways never before witnessed in the history of this land. We must not neglect this opportunity as Christians did after World War II, when General MacArthur pleaded for missionaries to be sent to Japan. Christians ignored that open door and squandered an opening that may not come again. We must not miss the opportunity that is before us in India. While the doors are still open, we must quickly spread the love of Jesus to the thousands who have never heard about His love for them or learned about His ability to forgive sin and restore lives. The doors are open, and the time to act is now.

By God's grace, we are trying to do our part to bring the message of hope and salvation to all who are lost. Indian Evangelical Team is the largest indigenous church-planting mission in India and also the fastest-growing mission in Asia, carrying the gospel of salvation to the villages of North India and bringing many souls into the kingdom of God.

Our current goal is to have 7,777 churches in Southeast Asia by 2010. People thought we were crazy when we announced a goal of planting 2,000 churches by the year 2000. But it was God's dream, not ours. There is a big difference between a "good idea" and a "God idea." One full year before the deadline, we had planted 2,254 pioneer churches.

We have been blessed by the good wishes and encouragement of the president of India, chief minister of Delhi, minister of State of Health and

Family Welfare, and other eminent national and international Christian leaders.

But tremendous need still remains. We continue to carry a great burden for the lost-and-hurting millions in our motherland and hope to see India evangelized in our lifetime. No one person can complete the assignment alone. But together, with God's help and leading, it can be done. The words Jesus spoke in Matthew 9:37–38 have never been truer: *"The harvest is plentiful, but the workers are few. Therefore beseech the Lord of the harvest to send out workers into His harvest."*

Prayer That "Works"

Certainly the wind of the Holy Spirit has begun to blow across the nation of India. Yet as you have learned, tremendous need still plagues the country. Do you sense the urgency of the situation? If you feel compelled to help, please keep in mind that mission organizations such as IET do have pressing physical needs, but first and foremost, they need *prayer*. If truth be told, earnest prayer is one of the greatest things you could ever do to meet the need.

Many times we blow off prayer because we do not understand its significance. But prayer is vital to the success of any Christian ministry. In fact, prayer is the key for unlocking God's abundant supply of the Spirit. When you pray, you release an activity, or energy, that goes to work in the spirit realm. You don't see that initial working with the natural eye, but you will eventually see its effect as you continue to pray and believe, expecting the Lord to work in the situation.*

The apostle Paul referred to this kingdom principle when writing to the church at Philippi from his prison cell. He said, *I know that this*

---

* Lynn Hammond, *Prayer Notes*, April/May/June 2008.

shall turn out for my deliverance through your prayers and the provision [supply] *of the Spirit of Jesus Christ* (Philippians 1:19). Paul was letting the believers know that their prayers had released an abundant *supply of the Spirit* that was working mightily behind the scenes. That supply had opened the door for the entire palace guard to hear that Paul was in chains for the cause of Christ. The supply was also hard at work in Paul's life, keeping him encouraged. And that supply was at work outside the prison as well, giving Christians newfound courage for speaking the word of the Lord boldly and fearlessly. (See vv. 12–14.)*

Peter was another great man of God who benefited from the effects of the Spirit's work as a result of earnest prayer. Herod the king had arrested Peter and was planning on putting him to death. Little did Herod suspect the formidable influence prayer would have on Peter's life-and-death situation! Acts 12:5 says, *So Peter was kept in the prison, but prayer for him was being made fervently by the church to God.* As fiery, faith-filled prayers went up, a mighty supply of the Spirit went to work on Peter's behalf. And, as always, the Holy Spirit knew just what to do. In this instance, He dispatched an angel to the scene. The angel woke Peter up, unshackled him, and told him to get dressed and throw his cloak around himself. The angel then proceeded to open every prison door, allowing Peter to pass through with ease and to walk out free and unharmed—without the guards ever seeing a thing (vv. 6–17).** What a picture of the power of impassioned prayer!

If God has touched your heart as you've read about the urgent needs in India, would you commit to praying for the precious people of this vast nation? Your prayers are indeed vital. Ask God for an abundant supply of His Spirit to "go to work" and unlock doors for those who are imprisoned by religious mindsets, unhealthy traditions, and demonic strongholds. James 5:16 says, *The effective, fervent prayer of a righteous man* [or

---

* Hammond, Prayer Conference in the Ozarks, 2007.

** Ibid.

woman] *avails much* (NKJV). Your prayers will make a lasting difference because in every sense of the word...prayer *works*!

> *Thank You, Father God, for the compelling assignment of prayer. I come to You now on behalf of the nation of India, standing in the gap for the people there. Continue to pour out Your Spirit across the land. From each bustling city to every mountain village and small community in between, may an abundant supply of the Spirit be released to work behind the scenes. Encourage the hearts of believers. Strengthen them and give them renewed courage to speak the Word boldly. Unshackle the captives and open every prison door that has hindered them from walking in the freedom Jesus provides. In His name, I pray. Amen.*

Chapter 14

MILLIONS ARE STILL WAITING

In the proportion that any of the disciples had means, each of them
determined to send a contribution for the relief of the brethren.
—Acts 11:29

IN 1996, I READ AN ARTICLE IN AN AIRLINE MAGAZINE ABOUT A
hidden tribe in Orissa called the Kui. Immediately my heart was
burdened for them, and I asked one of my leaders to gather some
information about these people so that we could begin an evangelistic effort there. The Kui tribe is the first of six people groups
discussed in this chapter—all of which give a glimpse into the soul
of India and the work that remains to be done.

THE HIDDEN PEOPLE

The Kui have a very primitive lifestyle, and they live deep within dense jungles. The men are short and strong, and the women disfigure their bodies with tattoos to deter outsiders from kidnapping or raping them. The people worship a sun god, mother earth, nature spirits, ancestors, and village dignitaries.

After some time, we were able to make contact with the Kui. It took two days of traveling by train, bus, jeep, and foot to reach the jungle interior where the Kui were spread out in various villages.

I slept on earthen floors with them, ate their food while seated on leaves spread on the ground, and bathed in the open stream while others guarded me from animal attacks. In the evenings, I shared the gospel with the people, and many opened their hearts and accepted Jesus.

The village chiefs observed my sincerity and expressed interest in knowing the true God who made the heavens and the earth. IET trained a few men in our Bible school and sent them back to reach their own people with the power of the gospel. Literacy classes were established, and after a few years, there were several thousand believers among this hidden tribe. In fact, two entire Kui villages came to Christ!

Recently one of my leaders asked if we could help with the costs of running a short-term Bible school. The doors are open, and God's heart is beating for the Kui.

WHERE OUTSIDE INFLUENCE IS ILLEGAL

The Bondo, a largely unreached people group, is a primitive tribe that lives outside the interior forests. Most of the tribesmen do not wear clothes, and when they dress, they wrap sheaths of wood and cloth around their waists. Killings and quarreling are common among them.

Because the Indian government has declared the Bondo a protected tribe, outsiders are not allowed to visit the tribal villages. As a result, the only time the Bondo people are usually seen is when they come down to the lower market to purchase goods from the villagers. Needless to say, the tribesmen are very wary of Christians approaching them.

Though it is illegal for a non-tribal person to influence the Bondo, Almighty God opened a way for us to get in through a man who speaks their language and works as a literacy teacher among them. This man initiated an outreach with the help of a woman whose mother worked in the government dispensary. The result was the first Bondo convert!

Recently, we were able to lead several Bondos in the lower region to the Lord, and four of those converts were brought to a short-term Bible school. Having never lived outside their tribe, two of them went back; however, in the case of the two who stayed, when their training was complete, they returned to the lower region to minister to their people.

Our future plans include expanding the work into the upper regions. My prayer is that the government will remove entry restrictions, along with the laws that forbid outside influence, so that we may openly send more workers to the Bondo people.

EARTHQUAKES ZIGZAG AROUND CHURCHES

When Dr. Ambedkar, the father of the Indian constitution, and 400,000 other Mangs chose Buddhism over Christianity, more than 100,000 people continued in their ancient faith, either as untouchables or as Muslims.

My heart went out to the Mang and Mahar untouchables. Many years earlier, Pastor John Osteen had donated forty thousand dollars to IET, which we used to hold forty gospel outreach meetings. As a result, over eighty churches were birthed. Then, in September 1993, a devastating earthquake pounded the area, killing thousands of people in a matter of seconds. One hundred seventeen villages were hit, but miraculously, the earthquake zigzagged around the eighty villages with the churches we had established, and the buildings remained unharmed.

One of the Mang missionaries asked me to send more men and finances. He assured me that if we could provide more workers and tools, at least five hundred more pioneer churches could be built.

FIVE SHAMANS FIND REAL POWER

The Savara are among the oldest of Indian tribes. They live in nearly inaccessible villages in the mountains between Orissa and Andhra Pradesh. The recent activities of terrorists with communist ideologies have made the entire area dangerous for outsiders.

Savara society is based on farming and hunting, and functional literacy is less than 10 percent. Before crops are planted, the village shaman worships the hill gods by offering liquor and sacrificing birds or goats.

The Savara see life as a harmonious relationship between the living and the dead. The gods and spirits make constant demands, and the Savaras care more about the malevolent spirits than their beneficial counterparts.

IET made a commitment to reach these remote people with the good news of Jesus Christ, and today hundreds of believers worship the true God in their own indigenous style.

Recently about two hundred men and women from various villages gathered in two jungle locations to renounce their pasts and publicly declare their commitment to Christ through baptism. Among the crowd were five shamans (holy men/witch doctors). As they reached the water's edge, the power of God hit them, and they were thrown to the ground.

Later they said, "If only we had known the truth when we were younger! But with whatever time we have left, we have only one desire—to take this light to every darkened heart."

What a testimony to the power of the living God to overcome the deepest darkness with the light of the gospel!

IET would like to build a Bible school for these people. At one point we had school in a local building in the region, but the owner of the building asked us to leave when he found out we were training men to preach about Jesus. Nevertheless, we believe our God will make a way!

A Unique Opportunity

There is a group of over 300,000 people who live in over one hundred villages in south central India. They are called the Kolam. In 1996, one of our mission leaders who was from this tribe (although from another state and language group), attended their annual festival. One of the chieftains who was quite old asked to meet with the IET missionary. After spending several hours with the missionary, the chieftain asked him to sit with him during one of the tribal meetings. It was an unprecedented move.

The missionary told me later, "Nothing like this has ever happened before. The chief has never let an outsider into the annual tribal festival or allowed anyone to sit with him."

The chieftain told him, "I am very old and may die anytime. But I want you to lead my people to prosperity in the knowledge of God." He then announced this to the 3,000 Kolams attending the festival.

A year later he invited me to meet him and speak to his people. After I preached, he blessed me and said, "IET shall carry on the work."

We have before us an open door and have appointed leaders to start a training center. These leaders have pleaded with me for evangelical tools, bicycles, and film equipment, and we are praying for provision to meet their needs.

Lost in the Desert

The Dhatki Bhils are spread over the desert region of India and Pakistan. Sixty-five percent are Muslim; the remaining are Hindu. The name *Bhil* is derived from the ancient Indian aboriginal word *billee*, meaning "bow," the traditional hunting weapon of the tribe. They are a semi-nomadic people, living in a barren and arid land, and they are very volatile.

The Dhatki Bhils were a completely unreached people group until 1999 when we tracked them down and sent missionaries to share the gospel. Faithful IET workers endured many hardships as well as the violent attitude of these anti-Christians who vowed to "kill the IET missionaries at first sight."

Today, almost a hundred Dhatki Bhils gather every week in a rented building to listen to God's Word. A literacy program has been started, but land is needed to build a worship center and start a school.

These are just a few examples of the wonderful people groups found in India. Our prayer is that God will meet our tremendous need for finances and resources so that we may reach out to these people and thereby fulfill the words of our Lord and Savior: *"Go therefore and make disciples of all nations, baptizing them in the name of the Father and the Son and the Holy Spirit"* (Matthew 28:19).

The needs are many, but our God is capable of meeting them all as His people are made aware and pledge to do their part. It is a job God has commissioned to each of us. Perhaps you would be willing to pray and ask our Heavenly Father what your part might be.

REACHING THE UNREACHED

Just as we at IET have established common ground with people groups by crossing cultural and physical boundaries to reach them, so the apostle Paul often gained an open door for sharing the gospel. He wrote, *For though I am free from all men, I have made myself a slave to all, so that I may win more. To the Jews I became as a Jew . . . to those who are under the Law, as under the Law . . . to the weak I became weak . . . I have become all things to all men, so that I may by all means save some* (1 Corinthians 9:19–22).

Can you identify? Are you so stirred with compassion for the lost that you constantly look for ways to establish common ground so that you can win them to Jesus—even those who are quite different from you?

Examine your heart today. If you find you lack passion for the lost or you need a strategy for reaching them, here are some simple steps to guide you on your way:

- Ask God to stir your heart for the lost.
- Establish common points of interest with the people God brings across your path.
- Pray for God to help you discover their spiritual condition.
- Ask for open doors to share your faith with those who don't yet know Jesus.
- Expect God to show up and show Himself strong.

Father, Proverbs 11:20 says, "He who wins souls is wise." Thank You for the unreached people groups IET is touching with the gospel. I want to be a soul winner too. Give me a burden for the lost in my own community, and lead me by Your Spirit in reaching out to them. Help me establish common ground and build relationships with those You bring across my path, and open the door for me to share the gospel with them. Then move, Lord, by Your Spirit to save them. These things I pray in Jesus' name. Amen.

Chapter 15

FRUITS OF OUR LABOR

God is not unjust so as to forget your work and the love
which you have shown toward His name, in having
ministered and in still ministering to the saints.
—Hebrews 6:10

IT WOULD BE IMPOSSIBLE TO RECOUNT THE STORY OF EVERY LIFE IET has seen changed for eternity by the transforming power of Jesus Christ. Each story is unique, each individual a walking testimony of a God *who desires all men to be saved and come to the knowledge of the truth* (1 Timothy 2:4). God will go to remarkable lengths to accomplish that goal! However, I would like to share a few specific stories with you that represent the impact of the work of God through IET.

Hindu Priest Becomes a Church-planting Leader

Kishan was the youngest of eleven brothers and sisters. His father was the most powerful Hindu priest in an entire cluster of villages. His magical powers had made him a powerful Shamaan, and his incantations could summon some of the highest demons to his service. In his search for even higher powers, he became a devotee of the bloodthirsty murdering goddess Kali.

It was evident that after the priest's death, Kishan would follow in his father's footsteps. In fact, the induction began when Kishan was just thirteen. During the day, a guru instructed the boy in Hindu rites and the basics of magic. But at night, the goddess herself would take his soul and teach him higher forms of magic and rituals while his body slept.

"It was very real," Kishan said. "I remembered the lessons and used the new methods with great results."

Even though he was still a young teenager, Kishan's fame began to grow. Then one day he saw a man standing by the side of the road, preaching about some God named Jesus. Kishan didn't understand what was being said, even when two women who had noticed him listening came over and explained the message to him.

Kishan didn't want anything to do with these Christians or their God. He made a vow then and there. "I will cut these Christians to pieces," he sneered.

That evening, when he was in bed but not quite asleep, a great light entered his room. Kishan instinctively knew that there was a person in the midst of the light. The light was so bright that Kishan had to shield his eyes. When he raised his head, he saw a tall stranger with a flowing, white robe and a kind face that radiated the glory of God. Kishan bent his head to shield his eyes from the light. He knew instantly that it was Jesus.

Kishan spat, "Why have you come here? I don't need You." Jesus stood silently. Kishan kept arguing with Jesus and asking Him to leave. "I have 3.3 billion gods and goddesses; why should I serve You?" he asked.

But there was no answer—just silence and radiant light. After midnight, exhausted from all his arguing, Kishan fell silent. Jesus spoke. "You are My beloved son."

"I don't know what happened," Kishan said, "but I began to weep and weep and weep. At some point I fell asleep, and when I woke up, I felt light and free!"

Kishan then ran to the IET members who had shared Jesus with him and began to devour the Word of God.

His family was aghast at what had happened, and they refused to allow him into their homes. The village chief said, "We won't give you any water." In an Indian village with only one well, the refusal of water meant excommunication.

But there was no turning back. Kishan had surrendered his life, and his only desire was to tell others about Jesus. "No one made me a Christian," he said. "Jesus Himself appeared to me. How can I forsake Him?"

Kishan left every morning to climb a new mountain and tell others about Jesus. He was often hungry, but he was determined to share the gospel with people in the different villages. He faithfully prayed for the various villages and for his family.

Miraculously, his stubborn family began to respond one by one. Today seven of his brothers and sisters have accepted Christ. A strong church of fifty baptized believers meets in his village, and two other churches have been planted nearby.

One day as he was walking on one of the high mountains, God spoke to him and said, "Look at the land. I will give you every village where you set your foot. I will make you a David."

Kishan continues his tireless work for the sake of the gospel. "I have been given this life to win the mountains of Sikkim for Christ!"

Persecuted for Christ

In June 2001, a three-day mini-crusade was conducted in Bihar, a state commonly known as "the graveyard of missionaries." During the crusade, a Hindu named Majhi heard the gospel message for the first time and immediately accepted Christ. When the IET evangelist who was leading the meeting began to pray for the healing of someone with severe pain in his lower leg, Majhi was healed instantly. He was baptized the next day in front of the villagers.

Then all hell broke loose. Majhi's family threatened him, his wife left him, and he became very sick. He grew so weak that he was unable to walk. But there was no one to help him—none of the Hindu villagers would have anything to do with him.

On the third day, Majhi was so hungry that he cried out to Jesus. Majhi says, "That night a stranger came and fed me a sweet porridge, and my strength returned. The next morning I was completely healed and as strong as ever." He hasn't been sick since.

Today, Majhi's wife has returned to him and become a believer. But the villagers have completely ostracized the couple and forbidden them to draw water from the only village well. This ill-treatment has forced Majhi's wife to walk a great distance to get their water. Nonetheless, Majhi is determined to stay and evangelize Bihar, the eleventh largest state in the country, where Christians are found in less than five of the people groups.

Buddhist Lama Converts

Sonam Lama was dedicated by his Buddhist parents to be a monk. He entered the monastery in Bhutan as a young child. He faithfully learned and chanted the mantras, often for hours every day.

When he was sixteen years old, tragedy struck. Blood began to flow from his mouth, and he became quite ill. The monks performed their rites and chanted mantras, but to no avail. His family sold most of their land to help pay for the powerful magic healers, but the situation didn't change.

Around this same time, an evangelist told the family about Jesus who heals. Sonam's family hated Christians, but unwilling to watch their son die, they agreed to let the evangelist pray for the boy.

Jesus healed the young Lama, which surprised him and caused him to want to know more about the One who heals. His father, satisfied that his son was well, wanted nothing more to do with Christians. After all, this was Bhutan, a Buddhist country, and becoming a Christian would mean not only losing honor but also suffering persecution. No one would marry his daughters, and his family would refuse to let him in their homes. He warned his son to keep away from the Christian missionaries.

But Sonam couldn't stop wondering why Jesus had died for him, as the missionary had explained. Compelled to know more, the young Lama accepted Jesus into his heart.

Needless to say, his family was furious. They refused to let him into their home. "You are dead to us," they told him. "Your name will never be uttered again."

When the monks found out that he had accepted Christ, they chased him from the monastery. That was thirty-five years ago, and Sonam has never been back. "They would kill me for sure," he says.

The former Buddhist Lama became a messenger of the gospel of Jesus Christ. He was threatened and thrown into jail. "Nothing could separate me from the love of Christ," he relates. When he was finally freed, he came to India where he now serves as a church planter among the Buddhists.

In 2002, Sonam Lama (renamed Daniel) moved to Romtek to fulfill IET's mission of reaching India with God's love. The Buddhist Lamas threatened him, but it was too late—Daniel had counted the cost. He refused to leave and continued to share about Jesus. Ever so slowly, people began to accept Christ, infuriating the locals and the monks.

As a result of Daniel's bold, unwavering commitment, a church was born. Today, about fifty believers attend the IET church, the only church in Romtek.

A Terrorist Comes to Christ

Sumer was a feared Bodo militant who had killed several people. His constant companions were his gun and alcohol. Every night, his wife would have to hide because he came home drunk. The bruises on her body spoke of her many beatings.

His parents had sold their land to pay Hindu priests to conduct prayers on their son's behalf, but nothing changed.

One day Sumer came home drunk and leapt toward his wife. She managed to wrestle free and run, but no one in the village would take her in. She finally reached the home of Manoranjan, an IET missionary who ushered her in and hid her from her furious husband.

Manoranjan and his wife gave the distraught woman their bed to sleep in and served her tea in the morning. She was deeply touched by the love of these Christians. When she returned home, she shared this with her angry husband. "Look at all the people you hate. Yet these people are filled with love."

In the evenings, Sumer and his friends would wield their guns and dance in the missionary's courtyard. But something about these people touched him. He was curious about the reason for the love they exhibited.

Later, he came back and listened carefully to the message the missionary shared. Soon after, he began to attend the IET church, the only church in the area, and there, he accepted Christ. His life was instantly and forever changed, an event for which both he and his wife are profoundly grateful.

Forsaking All to Follow Christ

Once when I was in Orissa, I went to a village called Gongall. There I met a young man who told me that his father was a Christian and his mother was Hindu. He said it was his father's deep desire to see a church built in the village before he died. In honor of his father's wishes, the young man gave us the land, and we built a church. Meanwhile, the man married, graduated from the university, and became a teacher. Because he'd grown up in a poor family, his burning ambition was to make a lot of money, live in a big house, and gain the social influence he'd never experienced in his youth.

Then one day he heard me preach, and he realized that even if he gained all the earthly wealth he could possibly amass, when the Lord required his life of him, he would be a poor man in heaven. He came and told me that he and his wife wanted to serve God.

They immediately resigned their jobs, and I asked them where they wanted to go. He said, "I'm from Orissa, and my father is from Andhra Pradesh, so I speak the dialects of each. My wife is from a nearby state and also speaks several languages."

I knew that Andhra Pradesh was well evangelized in the south, but not so much in the north. In the northern district, there is not much evangelization at all. In fact, one day as I was praying, I realized this pattern is true for most nations of the world. The southern regions are well evangelized, but not the northern regions. The young man and I talked a moment about this phenomenon, and he said, "I would like to go to the border of Orissa and Andhra Pradesh and evangelize the land because there is no preacher in the entire area, and my wife and I speak their languages."

I thought this was a good idea, so we commissioned this young couple to that area. The only house he could find was next to a leper colony. In fact, the room next door to him was occupied by lepers, but it was the only room he could get because he was a Christian.

Later, when I visited him, I cried. Truly, he has suffered more than any of us, including me. The whole area was filthy, and there were no toilets. It was the most disgusting place I had ever seen, and the stench was overwhelming. But God gave him an incredible increase! Today there are more than four hundred churches planted in the region! A Bible school has been established, and we are planning a children's home in the near future, as funds become available. In keeping with the ideology of IET, each person, with the Lord's help, is reproducing himself. If every believer produces another believer, every pastor another pastor, every church another church, eventually all of India will belong to the King and Creator of this world and the one to come.

We are continuing to send out missionaries to other regions of Andhra Pradesh where the work of God is not yet established.

All of this happened because one man heard the gospel and decided that he would rather have treasure in heaven, where moth and rust can't destroy, than to accumulate wealth on earth that will be blown away in an instant by the breath of God.

These amazing stories depict just five out of the thousands of lives in India that have been transformed by the power of God. I could easily fill a hundred books with such stories. There is no way to ever tell them all, but having spent more than thirty years traveling all over India, covering the entire northern region and pouring out my life to win people to the one true God through salvation in Christ, I can attest to the genuine transformations. At the present rate of conversion, we could quite possibly have a church in every village in every area.

Nonetheless, tremendous opposition to Christianity exists in the Indian government. In fact, officials have adopted the slogan "Protect the national religion" as part of their massive campaign to reconvert

Christians to Hinduism. Governmental authorities have implemented this crusade, using inducement, threat, and force. For example, if a person renounces Christianity, he will receive government benefits, but if he will not, the aid is withheld.

In another example, eighty thousand Christians were "reconverted" to Hinduism when one member of the militant Hindu political party known as BJP went into the villages with a gun and called the people out. He showed them his gun and asked for the Christians to step forward. The poor tribal people were terrified, so no one from any of the villages stepped forward. Then he sprinkled them with water from the Ganges River and declared, "From today on, you are a Hindu."

In another instance, over twelve thousand people in Orissa were "reconverted" when they were told their drinking water would be poisoned if they didn't refute Christianity and claim Hinduism.

So there is always more to do—more people to be reached, more lives to touch, more souls to be brought into the kingdom, more opposition to overcome—and we refuse to rest until all of God's purposes are accomplished.

LOVE IN ACTION

Are you compelled to be a soul winner? If so, then your lifestyle must "speak." Sometimes that means proclaiming the gospel with boldness, and other times it means extending the love of Jesus through acts of kindness. It's true that many people come to know Christ through anointed preaching. But it's also true that countless others receive Him because a believer first loved them unconditionally…and they were drawn to Jesus out of a curiosity about the amazing love they'd been shown.

Jesus said people would know we were His disciples by our love for one another (see John 13:35). In saying that, He didn't imply that we should only reach out to those who were easy to love. Rather, He called us to show love to all people, even the unlovely—those who are hard to get along with, those who reject us, those who are without hope, and, yes, even those whom society might consider outcasts or "untouchables."

Ask yourself today: Does my lifestyle speak? Do I share the gospel with boldness? Am I demonstrating the love of Christ to others, especially the sad and dejected? As you consider your need for increased boldness and more love for the unlovely, ask the Lord for the FAITH to believe He will:

- **F**orgive you for the times you didn't obey when He tugged at your heart to witness.
- **A**mplify your awareness that life is short, so every opportunity counts.
- **I**ncrease your anointing to share with boldness.
- **T**ranslate your behavior to communicate His unconditional love.
- **H**elp you to find the words when you don't know what to say and to demonstrate kindness when your actions would speak louder than words.

Father, today, I ask in FAITH that You will show me the people in my life who need You, and anoint and embolden me with Your message of love. Fill my mouth with Your words, and let my actions be a witness for Your kingdom even when my lips are silent. In Jesus' name, I pray. Amen.

Chapter 16

My Legacy in the Lord

I have been young, and now I am old; yet I have not seen the
righteous forsaken, or his descendants begging bread.
—Psalm 37:25

WHEN LILLY AND I DEDICATED OURSELVES TO BECOME FULL-time missionaries for the Lord, our families were sure that we would wind up in poverty and that our children would wear rags and be deprived of educational opportunities. In fact, Lilly's brother begged her not to resign her teaching position and follow her husband to the mission field. "Your children will be wearing second-hand clothes given by charities," he warned. "Our kids will have a good education and speak English, but your children will be forced to study with the poor kids in the regional languages. Our children will be well fed and healthy, while yours will be skinny and sickly."

The only thing I ever asked of the Lord for my family and myself was that my children would stand behind no one in Lilly's family or mine. I promised the Lord that I would never amass earthly wealth. My constant prayer was, "Lord, let my children be my wealth." I asked nothing more.

Recently a young man from the former Soviet Union asked if the Lord had ever failed me. "No," I answered truthfully, "He has never failed me." Not all of my prayers have been answered as I would have liked, but they have all been answered! In addition to the birth and ministry of IET, our greatest blessings have been our children. I am happy to report that our family's fears were totally unfounded. God continues to honor my request.

God Alone Accomplished the Unthinkable

None of my children have ever turned away from the Lord, even during their high school and college years. Four of the five are in full-time ministry.

Aby received his Bachelor of Science, Master of Divinity, and Doctorate degrees at Oral Roberts University (ORU) in Tulsa, Oklahoma. He and his wife, Babitha, a medical doctor, have two children. Aby and Babitha are involved in ministry in India—Aby preaching and Babitha using her skills to bring healing to the sick in central India.

Annie received her Bachelor of Science degree from Mount Carmel, Bangalore, and her Master's degree from Fuller Seminary. She and her husband, James, have two children. Annie is a family and marriage counselor, and James is a church planter in Gujarat, northwest India.

Blesson obtained his Bachelor of Business Administration Arts degree from Punjab and his Bible training in Sweden. He preaches in many countries and in various pastors' conferences in India. He and his wife, Rebecca, have one child. They concentrate their ministry in Europe and also travel often to the Middle East and India.

Grace received her Bachelor of Science degree from Mount Carmel, Bangalore, and her Masters of Divinity degree from ORU. Her only dream was to be a preacher of the gospel, and that dream has been fulfilled. She works in India, preaching with Lilly and me.

Ray received his Bachelor of Commerce degree in Bombay, and his Master of Business degree from ORU. He is presently praying for God's guidance in deciding the path of his life's work.

Truly, God has been faithful.

Lilly is busy traveling to different states, calling the wives of IET missionaries and the wives of lay preachers in our local churches, and conducting seminars. She also speaks in women's conferences and pastors' conferences.

Passing the Torch

Several years ago, the Lord showed me that I needed to begin preparing to hand the reigns of IET leadership over to a younger man. I knew that he needed to be a true visionary who shared my passion for winning the lost to Christ. After I had prayed and sought the Lord for quite some time, a young man came to mind.

Joy Thomas knew that he had a pastor's heart and felt his call was for a certain city, but I quickly began to take him with me wherever I went. There were several times when he asked me why we had to go all over India! But his desire to focus on a single city began to be challenged as we traveled to the different states and he saw the impact we were having on the entire nation. God expanded his vision, and it wasn't long before his heart was to win all of India.

In November 2004, when our dear brother Joy Thomas was ordained as the next president of the Indian Evangelical Team, the entire nation of India carefully scrutinized us. This was the first time that a man in India had planted a successful mission and then handed it over to someone other than a blood relative. In India, regardless of the type of work that is being continued, there is a dynasty mentality. Without exception, the work goes to a son, usually the oldest. There was tremendous pressure from many corners, and even from Joy, as we discussed whether I should select Aby to carry on the work. I refused.

Aby agreed with me wholeheartedly because he understood that God wanted to break the dynasty mentality and use IET as an example. When I told Aby my thoughts, without a trace of jealousy, he said, "It must not be from father to son, but from God's anointed to God's anointed. It's not enough that it be a good candidate. It has to be the right candidate—the one of God's own choosing."

We are convinced that God provided that man. Joy has no desire for earthly gain. He is willing to sacrifice everything in order to preach the hope of the gospel to those who are lost. I am quite sure that by the time Joy is my age, he will be much more mature and powerful in the ministry than I have been. Like a Joshua, he will carry on the task and complete the work that I could not do as he continues our vision of planting churches and establishing Bible schools.

God Is Faithful and Good

As has always been the case, IET must work hard to raise enough funds to pay its missionaries each month. Only by God's grace have we made it thus far. However, because He has blessed us with increase over the years, I would like to share the following example.

When I landed at Katra on November 6, 1972, I had 42 rupees in my pocket. When I passed the ministry to Joy Thomas on November 6, 2004, the total value of the land and buildings alone (including Bible schools, orphanages, and state headquarters) was 420,000,000 rupees. In addition, I had saved enough money to run the mission for at least a year so that Joy would not have to struggle. So, though we are by no means wealthy, we rejoice in God's bountiful goodness and His faithfulness to continue His work through us.

Presently, we are trusting God for help with an additional need. The father of our central office manager in Delhi came to us in 1977. At the time, he had an excellent job working as a mechanic for the government; however, when he came to talk to me, he said, "My spirit is restless. I want to do God's work."

I told him that he needed to think carefully about what he would be giving up and count the cost. I also reminded him that he had a good-paying job and a retirement pension, and that we could offer neither.

But he would not be swayed. "My mind is made up. I'm leaving," he insisted. Shortly thereafter, he resigned his government job, his wife quit her nursing job, and they both joined our team.

From the day this brother first came to us until now, he has proven to be a hard worker—but he's beginning to slow down a bit. Like our other aging missionaries, he has no savings, no insurance, and nothing of his own.

We have an obligation to help these people, and we have assured them that they will not be forgotten in their old age. We took care of them when they were active, and we will take care of them when they can no longer work. We could never abandon such wonderful servants who gave up everything to work for God in the mission fields of North India. So we are believing God yet again . . . that, in His goodness and faithfulness, He will supply the support to meet this important need.

Don't Count Me Out!

Although I stepped down as president of IET, I did not retire! My new position is "chief mentor" of the organization. There is still tremendous work to be done, and because I am now free from the demands of the office, I am able to devote more time to other needs. I travel to IET mission stations, conduct seminars for IET ministers, promote the ministry, and raise prayer and financial support so that the work of the kingdom can continue. I also have more time to write. I have a deep desire to write character studies on some of the great men of the Bible in order to encourage and equip the Church. In addition, I am now able to do further evangelistic ministry to fulfill the Great Commission.

I was pleased with the smooth transition and the witness it presented to a watching nation. I also am confident of God's hand on Joy and his wife, Elsie, and trust they will continue in their commitment to share the love of Christ...and take India for the gospel.

A Legacy worth Leaving

Always remember, the seeds you sow for the kingdom will produce a legacy of great value in the eyes of God. In essence, your legacy in the Lord will consist of the fruit that remains after a life well lived. Paul's words in Acts 20 depict a lifestyle that yields such a heritage:

> "And now I commend you to God and to the word of His grace, which is able to build you up and to give you the inheritance among all those who are sanctified. I have coveted no one's silver or gold or clothes. In everything I showed you that by working hard in this manner you must help the weak and remember the words of the Lord Jesus, that He Himself said, 'It is more blessed to give than to receive'" (vv. 32–33, 35).

When the Lord first moved on my heart to answer the call to share His love with the unreached of my beloved homeland, I was not thinking of the legacy I would leave behind. My only desire was to do His bidding. And even when I did question whether I would be able to leave any worldly possessions to my family if I became a missionary, I knew that to reject God's call would be to reject life itself.

Since those early days, the call from Luke 14:23, to *"go out into the highways and along the hedges, and compel* [the lost] *to come in"* has never ceased to reverberate in my heart and life. I do not brag when I say that I have lived a humble existence in an attempt to walk worthy of my calling. Nor am I prideful when I allege that I have laid down my own desires so that I might meet the needs of others. I am merely constrained by the call! As Paul so aptly put it, *"Yet when I preach the gospel, I cannot boast, for I am compelled to preach. Woe to me if I do not preach the gospel!"* (1 Corinthians 9:16 NIV). This is the legacy I leave—a life of sharing the gospel of the kingdom.

How about you? Have you considered the heritage you will leave? Take a few moments to think about the legacy you are presently creating:

- What words and actions are you sowing in the lives of your spouse, your children, or other members of your family?
- What deeds are you planting in service to the Lord?
- What acts of love have you shown a neighbor, a friend, or a stranger?
- With whom have you recently shared the gospel message of Jesus Christ?
- In what ways have you laid down your own desires to meet the needs of someone else?

No matter the call—whether to fulltime ministry, marketplace ministry, or ministry in your own home and family—I pray that you will sow the love of Jesus in the lives of others each day through your words and actions. In so doing, you will create a rich, lasting heritage, one that will continue to bear fruit for generations to come. Always keep in mind, if you sow kingdom seeds, you will reap a kingdom harvest...and that's *a legacy worth leaving*!

> *Father, I desire to leave a godly legacy. Help me to walk worthy of my calling. I declare Acts 20:24 and 27 over my life:*
> - *I will "not consider my life of any account as dear to myself."*

- *I will "finish my course and the ministry I received from the Lord Jesus—to testify solemnly of the gospel of the grace of God."*
- *I will "go about preaching the kingdom, not shrinking from declaring the whole purpose of God."*

Today I choose to die to self and lay down my life for others. Thank You for helping me to sow kingdom seeds that will produce a legacy of great value. I pray these things in the name of Jesus. Amen.

"Where Were You Half an Hour Ago?"

Years ago, as I was witnessing one day along the banks of the Hindu holy river, the Ganges, I sat talking with some Hindu holy men. During our conversation, I noticed a couple as they took turns showering kisses on their infant. I was particularly moved by the sight because most Indians don't show outward affection in public. But then, to my horror, in one swift motion, the man grabbed the baby and threw it into the swirling black waters of the Ganges River. The shrieks of the struggling infant were rendered silent as its tiny body sank into the river's icy grip.

Stunned and not quite believing what I had just witnessed, I ran toward the couple. The father was weeping, and the mother, overcome with grief, was pulling her hair.

In disbelief I stammered, "Was…was…that an accident?"

Between heaving sobs, the father cried, "No, I threw the child into the river."

I couldn't make sense of it. My first thought was that the child must have been born crippled or that they were getting rid of a baby girl, which is often the case in India. "Was the child a cripple...or a girl?" I asked.

The father shook his head, and in a grief-stricken voice, cried, "No, it was a healthy baby boy."

Incredulous, I asked, "Then why did you do it?"

"We have offered our child to the Mother Ganges to obtain salvation," came his heartbreaking reply.

"And did you receive your salvation?" I asked, my own heart broken over the needless tragedy and the only answer I knew he could give.

He shook his head and broke into a loud cry.

I stood helpless for a moment as he and his wife sobbed, and then I asked, "Have you heard about Jesus Christ?"

Thinking it was some kind of medicine that would calm his wife, he said, "I have never heard of this medication. Which shop can I find it in?"

After gently calming the couple, I shared with them the story of how God sent His only Son to die so that we could find forgiveness for our sins and true salvation.

They were shocked. The woman grabbed her chest with one hand, and with the other she pointed an accusing finger at me and shrieked, "If I had known this truth earlier, our son would not have had to die! Where were you half an hour ago?"

—

I have never forgotten that horrible and tragic encounter. It haunts me still. How many needless deaths could be avoided if only we could reach more Indian people with the life-changing message of salvation? The need is great and time is short. I am committed to working until the Lord calls me home, and will make every effort to reach people with the truth before it is too late. But I am only one man...and there is so much left to do. Would you pray and ask God how He would have you help in this mission? We need faithful people who will pray for the IET missionaries and pastors, and we also need funds to provide the needed ministry tools.

Please help us share the hope of the gospel with the hopeless souls in India... *before it is too late.*

Look What the Lord Has Done

IET Achievements

Year	Number of Workers	Churches Planted (cumulative)	People Baptized
1972	2	–	–
1973	2	1	10
1997	1,276	909	5,647
2000	1,793	2,988	12,700
2005	2,149	3,875	13,213
2008	2,406	4,496	6,116

Let us work together to evangelize India in our lifetime . . . and let us do it now!

If you would like to be a part of IET's mission work in India, please fill in the following form and mail it to the address below.

Yes, I would like to be a part of helping you reach India with God's love.

[ ] My contribution of $_____ is enclosed.

In addition, I pledge to:

[ ] sponsor a needy child for $20 a month.
[ ] sponsor a missionary for $50 a month.
[ ] sponsor a missionary family for $75 a month.
[ ] donate $3 for one Bible or $_____ for _____ Bibles.
[ ] donate $15 for one blanket or $_____ for _____ blankets.
[ ] donate $50 for one bicycle or $_____ for _____ bicycles.
[ ] donate $1000 for one motorcycle (for a missionary) or $_____ toward this fund.
[ ] donate $15,000 for one jeep (for a divisional leader) or $_____ toward this fund.

Name _____

Address _____

City _____ State _____ Zip _____

Country _____

Email _____

Please mail check and this form to:

Global Evangelical Team
P.O. Box 702411
Tulsa, OK 74170

Thank you for your generous support!